CW00544838

BRAND FART

Avoiding The 28 Common Branding Mistakes Photographers Make

by

Neo 'Norteyrazzi' Nortey

CONTENTS

FOUNDATION

The Search for Greatness: My Story

⌜ ⌝
⌞ ⌟

It's mid-2014, and life just wasn't going well for me. My long-term relationship with my girlfriend had recently ended and I had failed to break through into the acting and screenwriting industries, despite several years of trying. It felt like my dreams were slipping further and further away, and the frustration and disappointment were taking their toll.

I was in a dark place, emotionally, mentally, and financially. Depression had set in, and I was struggling to find my way out of the rut I was in. But then, something unanticipated occurred that would ultimately change my life. I stumbled across the well-known YouTube photography channel "DigitalRev TV" hosted by Kai Wong.

His enthusiasm for photography and his witty, humorous approach to teaching were infectious. For the first time in a long time, I found myself feeling inspired and motivated. Even though I had never owned a digital camera, I was immediately captivated by the art form.

As I soaked up the knowledge and insights Kai shared in his videos, it ignited a love for photography in me and I knew in my heart that I had found my calling in the creative industry. This discovery provided a ray of hope in a time of despair. However, I opted to follow a different career path at the time, and delayed pursuing my recently-discovered passion for photography.

Fast-forward to February 2019, when I told a friend of the family that I wanted to explore photography. She generously gifted me her unused Canon 1100D camera and kit lens, which became my entry into this exciting new world. I was beyond enthusiastic to begin my journey but also anxious because I didn't know much about the art.

As a person who is obsessed with greatness and with people who have maximised their creative and career potential, I was eager to study a household-name photographer who had achieved remarkable feats and whose work could serve as a source of inspiration. I was surprised to discover that I couldn't come up with a name off the top of my head. This realisation left me wondering why, despite photography being such a universally-used medium, it was so difficult to call to mind a legendary professional photographer.

I posed the same question to a few members of my family and close friends, but they too came up blank. Puzzled, this piqued my interest in the factors that go into making a name for oneself by excelling in the field of photography.

As I delved deeper into the subject, I came to understand that there is a significant distinction between fame and recognition as a household name. A household name, to my observation, is someone who has achieved greatness and whose accomplishments are acknowledged outside of their industry as well as within it. They are so exceptional that they have broken through glass-ceiling industry limitations or obstacles that can prevent most individuals from reaching the peak levels of success and admiration beyond their field.

On the other hand, being famous is more about gaining popularity and public attention, which is frequently accomplished through a combination of talent, charisma, and occasionally scandal or controversy. Being famous can lead to short-term success and accolades within a given sector, but it doesn't always translate into long-term impact or legacy outside that market.

To illustrate this point, I'll use the example of Michael Jordan and Tiger Woods, two athletes who have gained prominence due to their exceptional achievements in their respective sports. Having never watched either a basketball game or golf tournament, I'm very aware of Michael Jordan and Tiger Woods because of their accomplishments, and they are recognised worldwide as the greatest athletes in their fields. A household-name photographer, for instance, would have not only made significant contributions to the profession of photography but would also have had a broader impact on society, culture, and even history. It's a level of acclaim that transcends the industry and becomes a part of the collective consciousness.

However, despite photography's widespread use and influence, household-name photographers are hard to come by. In contrast to other creative industries where there are numerous examples of public figures, such as great musicians, actors, artists, music producers, DJs, chefs, and even doctors, the photography industry seems to lack comparable individuals. This realisation led me to question why photography, irrespective of its prevalence, has failed to produce many celebrated artists. It became clear that something was missing in how photographers promoted themselves and their work.

Since Joseph Nicéphore Niépce, credited with the invention of photography, developed the first successful photographic process in 1826, photography has permeated every aspect of modern life. It is used to capture memories, create eCommerce content, and even shape political and social movements. Despite this, it appears that achieving household name status is beyond the reach of even the most talented photographers.

Although becoming a public figure may not be the dream for every photographer, the absence of widely recognised figureheads has a detrimental effect on the entire photography community. Despite being an unquestionable art form, photography frequently falls short of earning the same respect and recognition as other creative fields. Due to the popularity of celebrity culture and social media influencers, photographers are frequently viewed as unimportant, with the focus being on the subject in front of the camera rather than the person behind it.

This became evident when I continually witnessed people failing to give credit to photographers by not tagging them when sharing their work on social media platforms. Furthermore, models and other individuals would re-edit images without consent in a way that altered the photographer's original vision, erasing the hours of work put in to create a particular aesthetic. The idea that photography is merely a tool for taking pictures rather than an instrument of creative expression is magnified by this lack of appreciation and respect for photographers, which erodes the value of their work and the art form as a whole.

In fact, the issue runs deeper and stems from the vastly held misconception that anyone can take a quality photo with the right equipment, which undermines the technical expertise, artistic ability, and innovative flair that photographers bring to their work. This devaluation of photography as a skilled craft has wider implications, fuelling a culture that undervalues and underpays photographers for their talent. Until photographers manage to shatter the glass ceiling of industry-imposed boundaries, their role in the creative process will continue to diminish and they will struggle to gain acclaim outside of the photographic industry and be valued for the significant impact they have on shaping our visual culture.

Upon reflection, it became evident that being a gifted photographer can only take you so far. To excel also requires being capable of successfully promoting and marketing yourself and your work to a broader audience. After acknowledging the importance of effective self-promotion, I began to analyse the photography industry and noticed a significant gap in branding among photographers.

Armed with this knowledge, I explored in greater depth the subject of branding and its relationship to photography. The further I went down this rabbit hole, the more it emerged that poor branding was responsible for the notion that photographers are merely the "face behind the camera" rather than the central focus... It became apparent that the problem that many photographers suffer from, from amateurs to seasoned professionals, is what I call "Brand Fart."

Brand Fart vs Brand Art

You just want to shoot and create pieces of digital art, I get it! As a photographer, your passion lies in capturing moments, playing with lighting, and crafting images that tell stories. Your work reflects your enthusiasm, skill, creativity, and artistic expression. Nevertheless, have you ever thought about your brand as a piece of art?

In today's world, it's not enough to just be a great photographer. With so many professionals vying for attention, it's crucial to stand out and create a strong brand identity. It's the initial impression you give to prospective clients, and it has a big bearing on whether or not they choose to work with you. Your brand is what distinguishes you from your rivals and serves as the voice of your business.

There are two directions you can go with branding: Your branding is either a hastily assembled Brand Fart or a masterfully created work of Brand Art.

Brand Fart

A Brand Fart has poorly executed branding that repels potential clients away from a photography business. It can manifest in different facets of your business, including your niching, messaging, pricing, marketing, and evolution, typically stemming from inadequate planning, scattered focus, and inconsistent use of various platforms. A photography Brand Fart often comes across as amateurish and implies a lack of attention to detail, which can turn audiences off. With an unclear message, strategy, and visual identity, it fails to captivate your target customer and hinders your success in an increasingly competitive industry.

Let's look closer at the areas where Brand Farts are typically found.

Brand Niching:
The process of identifying a particular market segment and tailoring your brand to suit its specific needs is known

as "brand niching." One of the biggest Brand Farts that photographers make is trying to cater to everyone and ultimately ending up appealing to no one. When you don't have a clear niche, and try to offer countless services, potential clients won't be able to identify what sets you apart.

Brand Messaging:

Your brand messaging should communicate your unique value proposition and how you solve your clients' problems. A Brand Fart in messaging occurs when your narrative is unclear, inconsistent, or irrelevant to your target audience. When your messaging is too generic, you'll struggle to attract clients as they won't understand why they should choose you over other photographers.

Brand Pricing:

A key component of your brand is your pricing strategy because it conveys your value to potential customers. A pricing Brand Fart photographers commit is setting their service rates too low or too high compared to their competitors, and not aligning their packages with their target audience's expectations. If you're priced too low, clients may perceive your work as low quality, and if you're priced too high relative to the value given, you may price yourself out of your market.

Brand Marketing:

Social media marketing is a vital feature of a photographer's branding strategy. However, it can also contribute to a Brand Fart if not executed properly. Potential customers may become confused and uncertain if your content is inconsistent with your brand, if you don't post frequently, or if you use a platform that doesn't connect with them. Similarly, relying solely on social media platforms as your portfolio and not having an optimised mobile-friendly website can hinder your business growth.

Brand Evolution:

Evolution is an essential aspect of branding for photographers. Your brand is not static and should evolve as your business grows and matures. However, a common Brand Fart photographers frequently make is failing to update their branding to reflect changes in their area of expertise, and not communicating those changes to their target audience. A photography business that fails to evolve its branding risks becoming dated and irrelevant, losing potential clients to competitors who better understand and reflect current market trends.

Brand Art

Avoiding a Brand Fart is crucial to the success of your photography business. To do so, you need to have a clear niche, consistent messaging, appropriate pricing, a strong digital marketing presence, and a willingness to evolve. Focusing on these aspects of your branding, planning, giving it detailed thought, and having a good understanding of your target market are the keys to a successful Brand Art. It embodies your unique value proposition as a photographer and showcases your originality, flair, and perspective. A consistent visual identity must be used throughout all of your platforms, such as your website, social media accounts, business cards, and advertising materials. It indicates your dedication to giving your customers outstanding service and how seriously you take your craft.

Identifying what makes you special, illustrating that you know your audience, and developing a brand strategy that defines your brand voice, brand values, and competitive advantages are all essential for building great Brand Art. Your brand should convey your narrative, evoke feelings, and forge a bond with your ideal market. It ought to reflect your brand personality, stand you out from your rivals and establish a level of confidence and credibility your target demographic has in your brand.

Let's look at the importance of Brand Art for photographers and how to use it to your advantage.

Making a Statement in a Crowded Market:
In the very competitive world of photography, Brand Art can help you stand out from the crowd. You'll draw

clients who are a good fit for your work ethic and style by building a strong brand that is genuine, represents your special talents, and is ultimately 'you'. You'll be able to explain to your market what sets you apart from other photographers and why they should pick you over them if you have a distinct and recognisable brand.

Increasing Visibility and Building Credibility:

You can increase your visibility and clientele by establishing a compelling Brand Art identity. By building a solid online presence through your website, social media, and other channels, you'll reach a wider audience and develop a reputation as a trustworthy and credible photographer. This is critical to gaining a devoted following, as clients are more likely to work with a photographer they perceive as professional and knowledgeable. Your brand should reflect your expertise, and you should consistently share your photographic wisdom and experience with your audience to reinforce your authority.

Providing a Sense of Direction and Purpose:

Defining your Brand Art can help you clarify your values, goals, and career path. By establishing a clear understanding of what you stand for and what you want to achieve as a photographer, you'll be able to stay focused on your goals and make informed decisions about your career. Brand Art can also help you stay motivated and inspired, as you'll know exactly what you're working towards and why it's important.

Building and Maintaining Relationships:
Brand Art can assist you in building and maintaining relationships with clients. By consistently communicating your brand values and mission, you illustrate your commitment to your work, which can lead to increased confidence and admiration from your clients. Additionally, strong Brand Art can assist you in developing a memorable customer experience, which is essential for building a positive reputation and attracting repeat business. You can establish long-lasting and fruitful partnerships with your clients by developing a relationship with them that is founded on mutual respect and trust.

Staying Relevant and Adaptable:
Brand Art is vital for staying relevant and adaptable in a rapidly changing industry. The business of photography is constantly evolving, and photographers need to keep up with the latest trends and technologies to remain competitive. By continuously building your Brand Art, you'll stay top-of-mind with your audience and be seen as a leader in your sector. You'll also be better equipped to adapt to emerging developments and innovations and pivot your business when necessary. With a robust brand, you'll have the foundation to evolve your business in

new and exciting ways to make sure you stay ahead of the curve.

In the fiercely contested photographic environment, your brand can mean the difference between success and failure. Understanding the difference between Brand Fart and Brand Art and avoiding the branding mistakes that photographers repeatedly commit will help you create a brand that resonates with your ideal client, fosters trust, and supports the growth of your career.

In the pages of this book, we will delve deep into how to avoid the 28 most common branding mistakes that photographers frequently make. We'll discuss the main distinctions between Brand Fart and Brand Art, providing thorough insights into each. Additionally, we will share examples from my journey and from reputable photographers who have proven the importance of Brand Art in their photography endeavours. Plus, we'll give detailed advice on how to develop a visual identity that is consistent across all of your platforms and marketing material. With this knowledge, you'll be able to establish a brand that sets you apart in a highly saturated industry, appeals to clients best suited to your photographic style, and helps in growing your professional business.

What a Photography Brand Isn't: Dispelling Misconceptions

You've probably heard a lot as a creative about the value of branding, but what exactly is a photography brand, and what can it do for your business? Here, we'll clear up some frequently held misconceptions about photography branding and provide advice on how to develop a stronger brand to set yourself apart in the crowded market.

Misconception #1:
A Brand is Just a Logo and a Website

One of the biggest myths about branding is that all it requires is a logo and a website. Even though these identity design blueprints are your brand's fundamental components, they don't entirely capture it. Your business, which encompasses everything your clients encounter, such as the calibre of your work, your customer service, your marketing material, and your social media presence, is how people emotionally perceive your brand.

Misconception #2:
Branding is Only for Big Corporations

Another widespread misunderstanding is that branding is only relevant to big businesses with big budgets. Branding is equally important for small companies, including photography businesses. Your brand gives you a competitive advantage over other photographers in your industry, and facilitates attracting and retaining clients. The key to effective branding is consistency, leaving a lasting impression, and forging an instantly recognisable and memorable brand identity.

Misconception #3:
Branding is Only About Attracting New Clients

While gaining new customers is important, a strong brand will also enable you to increase repeat business and form bonds with partners and clients. When customers are satisfied with your brand, they are more likely to refer you to others and use you again for their photography needs in the future. Building a reputation and gaining trust from clients and business associates are also important aspects of branding that will help your photography business succeed in the long run.

Misconception #4:
Branding is Solely About Standing Out

Although your photography identity should set you apart from your rivals, branding is more than just being distinguishable. It's also about communicating your message to your clients and partners about what your business stands for. This message needs to be genuine and reflect your beliefs, style, and special viewpoint as a photographer. Your target audience is more likely to remember you and hire you over other photographers if your brand narrative strikes a chord with them.

Misconception #5:
Branding is a One-Time Process

Developing a brand is a continuous process. Establishing and maintaining a solid, dependable presence in your clients' and partners' minds requires constant effort. Your brand should evolve as your photography business does. To reflect changes in your company or industry may entail updating your website, revising your marketing materials, or modifying your messaging. It's essential to regularly evaluate your brand and make any necessary adjustments to ensure that it remains relevant to your target audience.

Collectively Conscious Consumer Communities

In the age of social media, the landscape of branding has undergone a significant transformation. Previously, businesses of all sizes could shape their brand image through traditional, targeted marketing campaigns. However, with the emergence of social media and its universal usage, consumers now have the power to influence the perception of a company's brand.

Social media platforms have evolved into Collectively Conscious Consumer Communities, where opinions and experiences are shared, moulding the brand image of businesses before some individuals even have a personal encounter with them. This holds true for photography brands as well. The thoughts and impressions that consumers express about your creative brand, from customer service to online engagement, leave a lasting impact on others.

Photography businesses no longer possess the ability to control how individuals emotionally connect with their brands. The level of customer care and the brand message, however, are still under the oversight of photographers. By delivering exceptional service, going above and beyond, and maintaining a strong and authentic brand narrative, you can direct the general public's view of your business and establish a positive and memorable brand image in the minds of your target audience.

Whilst photographers along with all businesses are now incapable of dictating how their brand is perceived in this ever-connected digital landscape, you must recognise the power and potential impact of group judgement on your brand and take proactive steps to align your actions and messaging with your desired Brand Art. By actively listening and responding to both positive and negative feedback, you can address concerns, make improvements, and show your commitment to delivering exceptional experiences.

Dispelling misconceptions about photography branding is crucial for understanding its true value and the potential effects on your business. Although branding is often associated with big corporations, it holds equal importance for small creative businesses, providing a competitive edge and fostering client retention.

Your photography brand encompasses every aspect of your business that clients interact with and goes far beyond identity design elements, such as a logo and website. From the quality of your work to your customer interactions and online activity, your brand image is the personal relationship your audience has with your business. You must recognise the influence of collective brand perception and actively direct it through strategic actions and messaging.

Whilst standing out from the competition is important, effective Brand Art goes beyond that, communicating your authentic creative voice, values, and unique perspective as a photographer. By crafting a consistent and memorable presence, your brand becomes ingrained in the minds of your target audience. Keep in mind that branding is an ongoing process that requires continuous evaluation and adaptation to remain relevant in a dynamic industry. By dispelling these misconceptions and embracing the true essence of branding, you can position yourself for long-term success, establish your individuality, and form meaningful connections with your audience.

The Gap Between Who You Are and Who You Want to Be

You may feel inadequate as a photographer if you judge yourself against other professionals in the industry. However, developing your Brand Art is more about becoming the best version of yourself than it is about being the best in your field. To do this, you must bridge the gap between who you are and who you want to be.

To bridge the gap, there are several actionable steps that you can consider. These recommendations will help guide you on your journey of personal and professional growth, enabling you to develop your Brand Art and create a brand that truly reflects your vision and aspirations.

Define What Success Means to You:

You must be clear about your objectives if you hope to close the divide. Determine your definition of photographic success. Is it a steady flow of clients, having your work featured in a magazine, or a well-attended solo exhibition? You can begin pursuing success once you have a clear understanding of what it means to you.

Identify What You Need to Do to Achieve Success:

Establish what must be done to bridge the gap. This might entail making investments in your personal growth, developing a stronger portfolio, and networking and collaborating with other photographers and industry creatives. Setting clearly defined, quantifiable and doable objectives will help you move in the direction of whom you want to be.

Be Honest About Your Strengths and Weaknesses:

It's vital to be honest with yourself about your strengths and weaknesses as a photographer. Acknowledge your areas for growth and improvement, whilst also recognising and capitalising on your distinctive strengths and talents. By embracing your individuality and leveraging your competitive advantages, you can create a brand that authentically represents who you are and what you have to offer. This self-awareness will not only direct your branding initiatives but also help you differentiate yourself in a crowded photography market.

Stay Motivated:

The ability to maintain motivation is one of the biggest obstacles to closing the void. It's easy to become discouraged when you don't get results right away, but it's important to keep in mind that success requires perseverance. You can create a system of rewards for yourself to help you retain your enthusiasm, such as giving yourself some kind of a treat when you hit a certain milestone, or taking a break when you accomplish a particular goal.

Create a Support Network:

A solid support network is essential. This can include close friends, relatives, and other photographers who can support and encourage you along the way. Having a supportive and upbeat environment around you can help you stay focused and committed to achieving your objectives.

Be Patient:

It's important to exercise patience and to be kind to yourself. It takes time and diligence to establish your Brand Art, so it's critical to recognise and appreciate each small success along the way. Keep in mind that there will always be room for growth and improvement as you strive to maximise your potential. As you patiently navigate this path of self-discovery and brand development, trust that each step forward, no matter how seemingly insignificant, brings you closer to reaching your full creative capacity.

Understanding Your Unique Gifts

To successfully bridge the gap between who you are and who you aim to be as a photographer, it's fundamental that you acknowledge and maximise your special gifts and abilities. Each photographer possesses a distinct artistic vision, technical expertise and personal style that sets them apart from others. By identifying and nurturing these individual strengths, photographers can establish their identity, attract their target audience and achieve long-term success in the industry.

Here, we'll look into the importance of understanding your unique talents and skills as a photographer and provide valuable insights on how to harness and develop them.

Discovering Your Passion:
To understand your unique talents and skills as a photographer, it is vital to start with self-reflection and exploration of your passion. What aspects of photography ignite your enthusiasm and drive? Is it capturing landscapes, documenting people's stories, or exploring experimental techniques? Finding your true photographic interests allows you to tap into a source of inspiration that stimulates your imagination and serves as the basis for your unique aesthetic.

Recognising Your Style:

Style is a fundamental aspect of a photographer's identity. It encompasses the aesthetic choices, composition techniques, and emotional impact that define your work. Spend some time analysing your portfolio to find any recurring themes or elements. Do you gravitate towards bold hues or do you favour a more subdued, minimalist style? Does the mood in your work lean more towards drama or tranquility? By recognising and refining your visual trademark, you can attract clients who resonate with your artistic expression and create a recognisable brand.

Assessing Technical Proficiency:

In addition to artistic vision, proficiency in technology plays a crucial role in a photographer's skillset. Assess your current technical abilities and determine areas for improvement. Do you feel comfortable experimenting with various camera settings, lighting setups, and post-processing software? Continuously expanding and honing your tech capabilities not only enhances the quality of your work but also enables you to overcome challenges and capture the shots you envisage.

Leveraging Your Personal Experiences:

Your life experiences and background bring a unique perspective to your photography. Think about your personal journey and how it can influence the way you tell stories with photographs. Whether it's your cultural heritage, travel experiences, or individual interests, incorporating these elements into your work adds depth and authenticity. By sharing your distinctive viewpoint, you can create meaningful connections with your audience and differentiate yourself in a crowded market.

Being Money-Motivated

In the business world of photography, it's not uncommon for photographers to be enticed by the allure of financial success and the desire to be rich. However, focusing solely on monetary gain can have adverse effects on the development of your Brand Art.

Here we will explore the reasons why photographers driven by money often end up with a weak brand identity and the other potential pitfalls associated with this mindset.

Sacrificing Artistic Vision:
When photographers are primarily motivated by money, they may find themselves compromising their artistic vision and creative morals. The pursuit of financial gain can lead you to deviate from your personal expression and originality and fall victim to the pressure of replicating popular styles or conforming to fashionable market trends. This concession dilutes the uniqueness of your photographic work, blurring your brand message, and

diminishes your ability to leave a lasting impact on your audience.

Neglecting Authenticity:
   Photographers who are motivated by money frequently put money before authenticity. In their quest for profitability, they may take on projects or clients that are in conflict with their artistic values or personal interests. This can result in a disconnect between you as the photographer and your artwork, leading to a lack of passion and integrity in your portfolio. Clients are drawn to photographers who genuinely connect with their craft and deliver a unique perspective. A weak brand identity emerges when you fail to convey your true creative voice.

Chasing Quantity Over Quality:
   A primary focus on money can lead photographers to prioritise quantity over quality. They may be tempted to cast a wide net, offer a broad range of photography services, and take on numerous assignments without dedicating enough time and attention to each project. The quality of your work may suffer as a consequence, and you risk developing a reputation for producing inconsistent photographic work. This compromises your brand's credibility and fails to inspire trust and confidence in potential clients, resulting in a weakened brand persona.

Superficial Client Relationships:

When the main objective is monetary success, photographers may prioritise financial transactions over cultivating meaningful relationships with their clients. This approach can result in a purely transactional and impersonal experience for customers, triggering a lack of loyalty and repeat business. Building a strong bond with the individuals who hire your services is essential for your photography company to thrive, as it fosters trust, word-of-mouth referrals and steady growth.

Being the "Best"

In the creative industry, many individuals aspire to be acknowledged as the "best" in their respective fields. While pushing for excellence is admirable, the notion of being the absolute best is subjective and elusive.

The world of sports provides clear criteria for measuring superiority, such as winning tournaments or setting records, making it relatively simple to identify who holds the coveted crown. For instance, in athletics, the athlete who runs the fastest and wins the 100-metre sprint final is considered the best. Similarly, in boxing, the best boxer in the ring following a title fight is the one who wins by knockout or on points after 12 rounds. However, the idea of the best is open to interpretation and personal preferences within the creative industry, spanning photographers, artists, actors, and musicians.

Even prestigious awards and accolades, like the Academy Awards or the Grammys, are subject to the opinions of a selected committee. Different panels or judges might yield contrasting results, highlighting the personal nature of determining who's the best.

Furthermore, attempting to measure greatness solely by financial prosperity or online popularity is inherently flawed. While monetary gain and a large following on social media can be indicators of success, they do not necessarily capture the essence of mastery of a craft. Some artists may have a well-established commercial cash machine behind them, marketing their work to a wider audience and generating substantial revenue. Whilst an exceptionally talented creative, despite their outstanding abilities and noteworthy contributions to the industry, may remain relatively unknown and struggle to garner widespread recognition and significant wealth without comparable investment and support.

Art, by its very nature, is art. It's neither good nor bad. Its appreciation is deeply personal to those who engage with it. This makes the notion of being the "best" in the creative industry subjective and impossible to define, as it lacks a universally accepted framework. This ambiguity stems from the multitude of perspectives and evaluation criteria used to assess excellence within an artistic discipline, rendering the attainment of a widely agreed-upon status as the unquestionable best in any specific domain a futile pursuit.

Instead of fixating on being the best, focus on your personal growth and continuous improvement. If you seek to be better than another photographer, then you ultimately lower yourself to be measured by their standards. Strive to become the greatest version of yourself as a photographer. Embrace your unique vision, style, and artistic voice. Push your creative boundaries, experiment with new techniques, and refine your skills. When you are authentic to what makes you tick as a creative, you become irreplaceable, because there will never be another "you". Your ultimate objective should be to make a lasting impression, produce meaningful work, and experience contentment in your artistic journey.

Keep in mind that true success as a photographer is measured by personal satisfaction, progression, and the ability to connect with others through your art. Value the process of perfecting your craft, pursuing your passion, and making an influential contribution to the world of photography. In the end, it is the fulfilment of your creative potential and the impact you make that truly matter, rather than craving the unattainable title of being known as the best.

While financial success is a legitimate goal, photographers must be cautious about becoming solely money-motivated. By prioritising monetary rewards above all else, you risk developing a Brand Fart image characterised by a lack of authenticity, inconsistent quality, an absence of focus and a difficulty in building meaningful client bonds. To establish a positive brand image, you must strike a balance between financial goals and the pursuit of artistic excellence, creativity, and client-centricity. By staying true to your unique vision, delivering exceptional artwork, and fostering customer relationships, you can create a powerful and enduring Brand Art that transcends monetary aspirations.

Being a photographer requires you to go on a journey of self-discovery and ongoing development. You can build a solid foundation for your Brand Art by acknowledging what inspires you, recognising your style, honing your technical proficiency, and drawing on your personal experiences. Understanding and embracing your special talents will help you to bridge the gap between who you are and who you aspire to be, and position yourself as a distinctive and valuable photographer in the industry. Prospective clients are drawn to photographers who have a clear artistic vision and can provide a unique perspective through their work. You will distinguish yourself from the competition by effectively communicating your style and showcasing your abilities.

Discovering and appreciating your unique photographic gifts and skills not only brings a sense of fulfilment but also allows you to create work that is authentic to who you are. By recognising your strengths and setting clear objectives, you can strive to embody the highest calling of your creative self. When your passion and artistic expression align with your photography, it opens the doors to a pleasurable and enriching career. The satisfaction that comes from producing work that is true to yourself and resonates with others is unquestionably priceless. With the drive to close the gap to who you desire to become, celebrating your individuality and allowing it to shine through your imagery, you'll have the power to create significant and impactful visual art that leaves a lasting imprint on those who interact with your creative work.

BRAND FART NICHING

⌐ ¬
⌐ ¬

In today's competitive photography market, it's more important than ever for photographers to establish a unique brand identity that differentiates them from their competitors. One of the biggest mistakes that photographers make when developing their brand is attempting to be a jack of all trades and catering to every conceivable client. Offering a wide range of services may seem like a good idea to appeal to a broader audience, but this Brand Fart strategy can ultimately result in a diluted brand reputation and make it difficult to carve out a marketplace for your photographic business.

To succeed in the business world of photography, you must identify your niche. In essence, your niche is a narrow area of specialisation for your creative enterprise that enables you to stand out from industry rivals and concentrate on a particular clientele. It requires locating the intersection of your interests, abilities, and a market need that you can fill.

In my experience, discovering my niche was a process of trial and error. I began by shooting everything, from fashion, products, and landscapes, to events, as most new photographers find themselves doing. However, as my skills improved and my social media following grew, I began to receive requests from modelling agencies to shoot fashion photography for their recruits. This eventually led to a turning point in my journey when a model asked me to do some implied shots, which sparked my passion for boudoir photography.

It was during this transformative experience with boudoir photography that I recognised the immense power of capturing intimate moments and celebrating individual beauty. This revelation served as the catalyst for my decision to specialise in this genre and develop a platform where women could authentically express their confidence and embrace their unique identities.

As someone passionate about greatness, I have always had the rare ability to spot raw potential in people, particularly those in creative fields. My new shift in focus towards the art of boudoir led me to explore talent in the world of modelling, and I quickly realised that many young women could make incredible models but were being overlooked by the industry and other photographers.

Using this innate gift, I began actively scouting on social media and in person for models with special features that could be captured in a photo and used to launch a modelling career. Many of these women were regular people who may not have fit the typical mould of a professional model, but whose distinctive appearance and spark of greatness caught my attention.

I began working on my personal photoshoot projects with these models, showcasing their talent and beauty in a manner that they had never seen before. By capturing their individuality and sensuality in boudoir photographs, I created a niche for myself in the industry.

Collaborating with largely undiscovered models gave me a notable edge in the highly competitive field of photography, enabling me to infuse a distinct outlook into my photoshoots and images, and deliver an innovative experience to my clients, which became known as "The Nortey Experience". The models I worked with were not well-known in the business, nor did they have a large social media following, but their striking looks and fresh energy connected with audiences in a way that today's conventional models simply could not.

I witnessed these women blossom into empowered, self-assured people who were eager to pursue modelling as a profession whilst I continued to work with them. I earned a reputation as a photographer who could identify potential and support the launch of new models' careers. Many of them went on to make a name for themselves in the industry, and I am honoured to have played a role in establishing their professional path. My ability to spot and unearth gifts in others and help them achieve their creative goals within the industry has been one of the most rewarding aspects of my journey as a photographer.

As I embraced my niche, I was able to leverage it to open up new doors and opportunities. By positioning myself as an expert in launching new faces and specialising in boudoir photography, I was able to attract and work with some of the best models and boutique brands, as well as travel throughout Europe. This is the power of Brand Art niching.

For your Brand Art, it's important to remember: your niche should be determined by both your interests and market demands. You want to find a balance between what you love to shoot and what appeals to potential clients.

Once your niche has been established, you must build a solid brand identity around it. Your brand should be consistent throughout all of your marketing materials and reflect your distinct sense of style and personality. This includes your website, social media profiles, and business cards. Your brand should be instantly recognisable and convey the value that you offer to your clients.

As we explore the advantages of brand niching, we'll provide practical advice to help you find your unique niche and position your brand for success. Whether you're a novice or an experienced pro, this chapter will help you avoid the Brand Fart pitfalls and create a solid framework for your photography business.

FART/1:

Trying to Appeal to Everyone

You possess a remarkable talent for capturing the essence of a subject in a single frame. However, having a good eye and strong technical skills are not the only things necessary to build a successful photography company. In addition to this, you need to be familiar with the value of niching, as well as how to implement the concept into your photographic strategy. By understanding the importance of pinpointing your area of expertise and designing your services to meet the unique needs of your market, you can develop a positive brand image and attract the right clientele for your business.

While the concept of identifying a niche and targeting a specific audience is widely advocated in the photography industry, it is important to acknowledge why some photographers choose to take the Brand Fart approach and serve everyone. Although this practice may seem appealing at first glance, it is vital to understand the potential pitfalls and challenges it can bring to your branding efforts.

Here we will look at some of the common reasons why photographers choose to please everyone despite the drawbacks.

Fear of Missing Out:
One reason photographers choose to serve everyone is the fear of missing out on potential opportunities. They worry that by narrowing their focus to a specific niche, they may limit their chances of attracting clients and booking diverse projects. However, it's essential to recognise that attempting to cater to everyone often leads to weak branding and a lack of clear differentiation in the market. Without a distinct identity and area of expertise, it becomes difficult for prospective consumers to understand what sets you apart from other creatives.

Variety and Flexibility:
The desire for flexibility and variety in their work is another reason why some photographers choose to serve every conceivable individual. They see the challenge of working on various projects as a way to maintain their creativity. However, the downside of this approach is

that it can result in an inadequate level of specialisation and mastery. Without a clear focus, you may struggle to establish a strong brand identity and distance yourself from industry competition. Clients seeking a particular aesthetic or expertise are more likely to gravitate towards photographers who practise in their desired niche. By trying to be versatile in all areas, you risk diluting your skills and compromising your ability to deliver exceptional work in any specific genre.

Building a Diverse Portfolio:

Building a diverse portfolio is often seen as an advantage of trying to fulfil the photographic needs of everyone. Photographers think that showcasing their diversity and range of skills can draw in a broader clientele. While having an extensive portfolio can illustrate adaptability, it can also create confusion for prospective clients. Without a clear niche, it becomes challenging for customers to identify your unique strengths and understand how you can specifically meet their needs. Clients are attracted to creative individuals who specialise in their desired genre or style, as it gives them confidence in the photographer's experience and the ability to deliver on their expectations.

Personal Fulfilment:

For some photographers, serving everyone and capturing a wide variety of moments and stories brings them personal fulfilment. They relish the chance to interact with various people and communities and derive meaning from the diversity of experiences they encounter. However, from a branding perspective, this approach may hinder your ability to establish a clear and compelling brand identity. Clients are more likely to connect with photographers who have a distinct target demographic and exhibit a passion and understanding for what they deliver as a visual creative. By focusing on a particular niche, you can cultivate a unique brand that attracts an audience that admires your specialised skills and photographic philosophy.

In the rapidly-evolving photography industry, trying to appeal to everyone is a Brand Fart that can hinder your growth and weaken your brand identity. Adopting the concept of identifying your niche allows you to carve out a unique space for yourself, attract the right clients, and establish a favourable brand image. By understanding your signature talents and skills as a photographer and crafting your services to meet the needs of a specific demographic, you position yourself for success in a competitive market.

It's important to remember that finding your niche is not about setting boundaries for yourself, but rather about concentrating your efforts and resources to provide first-class services and results in a particular field. Create a Brand Art that resonates with your target audience by embracing your passions and developing your expertise. In doing so, you will attract customers who appreciate your special abilities and gifts, leading to a fulfilling and prosperous photography career.

SUMMARY:

FROM FART TO ART

Brand Fart

While the desire to appeal to everyone may stem from good intentions such as broadening opportunities, enjoying flexibility, building a diverse portfolio, or finding personal fulfilment, it is vital that photographers recognise the negative impact it can have on their branding efforts. By diluting your focus and sacrificing differentiation, you run the risk of developing a vague, forgettable photography brand, leading to a decline in demand for your services.

Brand Art

Successful photographers understand the importance of defining a niche, targeting a specific audience, and developing a strong brand identity that resonates with their ideal clients. By focusing on and catering to a particular market segment, you can position yourself as the go-to photographer in your field, establish a reputation for delivering customised services and, ultimately, differentiate yourself from competitors.

FART/2:

Underestimating the Power of Specialisation

In the world of photography, it can be tempting to try your hand at everything in the hopes of attracting more business. However, this Brand Fart strategy frequently produces subpar results and leads to failure. The key to creating a successful photography Brand Art is specialisation.

The term "specialisation" means concentrating your knowledge and abilities on a narrow area of the photography market. This could be anything you are passionate about, such as boudoir photography, street photography, food photography, or another niche. The key is to identify your area of expertise and become an authority in it.

Whilst it's natural to worry that narrowing your focus will limit your potential client base, not specialising can be even riskier. Offering too many services could cause you to become overburdened and unable to deliver the best results in each area. This Brand Fart may end in a drop in work quality, a decline in customer satisfaction, and a poor reputation.

On the other hand, specialisation enables you to provide your clients with a service that is more focused and tailored. This distinguishes you from other photographers and draws clients who are looking for a specialist in their particular field of interest. You can establish credibility within your domain of expertise by concentrating on a specific niche. If you can convince clients that you are an authority in your discipline and can deliver exceptional results, they will be more likely to recommend you to others.

One photographer who has successfully utilised this approach is Brandon Woelfel. He has effectively developed a distinctive and recognisable personal brand using his unique style of dreamy, surreal photography, which incorporates colourful lights and bokeh. He has established a brand that is instantly recognisable as being his own by developing and maintaining a consistent visual aesthetic.

By specialising in creating a specific type of portrait imagery, Brandon has been able to confine his focus to a particular class of clients and collaborations. He works with brands that are renowned for their inventive and creative marketing strategies, such as Urban Outfitters, Bose, and Apple. By associating with this calibre of companies, Brandon has been able to strengthen his Brand Art, amass a devoted fan base, and broaden his reach to new audiences.

Identify Your Specialisation

Identifying your specialisation plays a vital role in establishing your photography business. Here are some key steps to help you define your niche and set yourself up for success.

Reflect on Your Photographic Inspiration:
Take the time to reflect on the aspects of photography that truly ignite your passion and bring you joy. Consider the subjects, genres, or styles that resonate with you the most and allow you to express your creativity and photographic abilities to the fullest. Your area of specialisation should align with your genuine interests, as it will fuel your drive and enthusiasm to excel in your chosen discipline.

Assess Your Expertise and Experience:

Self-evaluation of your skills, knowledge, and experience in various photography fields. Identify the areas or subjects in which you have the most expertise and consistently deliver exceptional results. These are the genres where you can showcase your unique talents and differentiate yourself from others in the industry. Your specialisation should leverage your existing artistic strengths and allow you to establish yourself as an expert in your designated domain.

Define Your Target Audience:

Once you have identified your area of speciality, it's crucial to define your market within that sector. This requires taking into account the characteristics, preferences, and desires of the specific clientele or demographic you wish to serve. For instance, let's say you have chosen wildlife photography as your specialisation. Your target audience within this niche might include nature enthusiasts, wildlife conservation organisations, wildlife destination travel agencies, or publications focusing on wildlife and nature. By understanding your ideal customer, you can tailor your services and messaging to effectively resonate with them, positioning yourself as the go-to photographer in that particular market segment.

Test and Refine:

It's important to test your creative ideas and gather feedback after determining your potential niche and desired audience. Offer your photographic services to a select group of clients within your target demographic and pay attention to their responses. Evaluate their satisfaction, referrals, and repeat business to gauge the success of your specialisation. Use constructive criticism from your customers to understand what is working well and where improvements can be made. Use this information to refine and adjust your niche if needed. Continuously track and analyse the success of your chosen photography speciality and make necessary modifications to ensure it remains aligned with market demands and your own professional goals.

Another advantage of specialisation is the ability to effectively concentrate your marketing efforts. By narrowing the scope of your marketing initiatives, you can connect with a more relevant and engaged audience. This increases the effectiveness of your marketing campaigns and ensures that the appropriate audiences are hearing what you have to say. If your area of expertise is wedding photography, for instance, you can focus your marketing efforts on newly engaged couples who ultimately will begin searching for a wedding photographer in preparation for their big day.

It's important to remember that diversifying your services is not prohibited by specialisation. You can think about extending your services to related fields once you have built up your reputation and brand identity within your niche. Using the example of a photographer who specialises in wedding photography, you might also offer engagement and destination wedding photography as well as pre-wedding photoshoots. By doing this, you can expand your clientele and your business while keeping your skills and attention strictly focused on your area of expertise.

Keep in mind that specialisation is not a one-time decision. You might need to reevaluate your niche as your company expands and matures to make decisions that will keep it profitable and relevant. But by remaining committed to your region of speciality and consistently improving your abilities, you can position yourself as a top expert in your field and create a photography Brand Art that flourishes.

FROM FART TO ART

Brand Fart

Neglecting the power of specialisation in photography can result in detrimental consequences for photographers. Failing to appreciate the importance of honing in on a specific niche can lead to a weakened brand identity and insufficient expertise. When you try to serve a broad range of customers and cover various genres, you will ultimately struggle to make your mark in the industry amidst fierce competition and fail to attract your ideal clientele.

Brand Art

By recognising the importance of specialisation and taking intentional steps to identify and embrace a niche, photographers can set themselves up for success, stand out from the crowd and build a thriving business that aligns with their passions and expertise. Specialisation allows you to focus your energy and resources to become an expert in your field, and to attract clients who value your unique skills and photographic services.

FART/3:

Failing to Define Your Unique Value Proposition (UVP)

It can be challenging to set yourself apart from the competition in the congested photography industry. Since digital cameras and smartphone cameras are so widely available, anyone can technically identify as a photographer. However, to differentiate and make a name for yourself in the industry, you need a unique value proposition (UVP).

The distinguishing characteristic that makes you stand out from your rivals is your UVP. It influences clients to pick you over competitors. Without a clearly defined UVP, you expose yourself to the danger of becoming one of the crowd, which will make it difficult to attract and retain clients.

Many photographers mistakenly believe that their technical skills, their camera gear, or their years of experience in a particular sector are enough to draw clients' attention. However, in today's market, it takes more than that. Clients are looking for something that speaks to them on an emotional level, something that they can connect with. That's where your UVP comes in.

Your UVP should be a combination of your unique skills, personality, and the specific type of photography that you are proficient in. If you specialise in fitness photography, for instance, your UVP might be that you excel at capturing the strength, dedication, and transformation of individuals through captivating fitness imagery. By understanding the dynamics of fitness, the human body, and the essence of athleticism, you distinguish yourself from other fitness photographers who may only focus on the technical aspects of photographing their subjects.

To develop your UVP, ask yourself the following questions:

- What sets me apart from other photographers?
- What special skills or techniques do I offer my clients that distinguish my photography?
- Who is my ideal client, and what are their needs and preferences?

- How can I effectively communicate my unique value proposition to potential clients?
- What kind of results can clients expect from working with me, and how do I follow through on my promises?
- How do I measure the success of my UVP and make improvements over time to meet changing client needs?

Once you've answered these questions, start to formulate your UVP. Remember that your UVP needs to be memorable, clear, and concise. It should convey the essence of your brand as well as the advantages you offer to your customers. Avoid using technical terms or industry jargon in your UVP as it could turn off or alienate potential clients.

You must make sure that your UVP is evident in everything you do for it to be effective, from how you conduct business to how you present yourself and your work. Ensure that your UVP is clearly communicated on your website, portfolio, and social media profiles. By doing this, you'll be able to draw in the right clients and maintain the consistency of your brand across all channels.

Here are a few examples of Brand Art UVPs:

Fashion Photographer:

"I specialise in capturing fashion that tells a story. My unique approach combines creativity and technical expertise to produce images that convey the personality and aesthetic of each brand or designer, assisting them in standing out in a competitive industry."

Music Event Photographer:

"I capture the heart-pumping energy and raw emotion of live music performances through dynamic, visually stunning images that transport viewers straight to the soul of the event."

Product Photographer:

"I specialise in creating captivating images that showcase the essence and features of your product. With a keen eye for detail and a focus on your brand's identity, I deliver exceptional visuals that engage your audience and elevate your online presence, helping you establish a competitive edge in the marketplace."

Keep in mind, as you gain experience and as your clients' needs change, your UVP will continue to evolve. But defining your UVP is a crucial first step in creating a lucrative photography business. It helps you to differentiate yourself from the competition, attract the right customers, and keep your brand consistent and memorable.

Additional pointers to help you develop your UVP over time:

Examine Your Rivals:
Look at other local photographers and see what they are doing. This will assist you in locating market gaps and ways to set your UVP apart from the competition.

Concentrate on Your Target Market:
Your UVP should be tailored to appeal to your niche. Think about the desires your target audience seeks in a photographer and how you can offer those qualities distinctively and memorably.

Experiment Without Fear:
Don't be afraid to try new things and experiment with various approaches, because your UVP should be an expression of who you are as a photographer. This can help you figure out what works best for you and your clients.

Get Feedback:
Ask for feedback from your clients, colleagues, and mentors. You can use this to pinpoint your UVP's advantages and disadvantages and make the necessary corrections.

Remember that your UVP is a reflection of your identity as a photographer, not just a marketing tool. You can attract the right customers, develop a long-lasting and successful business, and establish a Brand Art you can be proud of by taking the time to define your UVP and evolving it over time.

FROM FART TO ART

Brand Fart

Photographers without a UVP frequently have a vague or generic message that falls short of differentiating them from their rivals. Potential clients may find it challenging to understand what makes you unique and why they should pick you over other photographers as a result.

Brand Art

Proficient photographers identify their unique value proposition that speaks to potential clients on an emotional level and sets their business apart from its competition. Your UVP should be memorable, clear, and concise, and should convey the essence of the brand as well as the advantages it offers to clients.

FART/4:

Failing to Clearly Communicate Your Niche Market

To develop your Brand Art and gain a competitive edge in the photography industry, one of the most important steps that a photographer can do is to identify their niche market. However, one common mistake is failing to communicate their niche market once it has been determined, which can negatively impact the success of their brand.

Defining and communicating your area of specialisation is one of the key factors to building a successful Brand Art as a photographer. By doing so, you enable potential clients to easily understand what you do and whom you serve. As an illustration, take the work of photographer Brandon Woelfel, who has mastered his surreal style and inventive lighting techniques over the years to effectively communicate his niche market.

By articulating his niche through his visual aesthetic and online presence, Brandon has attracted a particular audience that values his distinctive approach to photography. Brandon has built up a large community on social media with 2.3 million+ followers on Instagram and over 500K subscribers on YouTube, where he frequently posts about his work, creative process, and day-to-day activities as a photographer. By doing so, he skillfully conveys his niche market, differentiates himself from competitors, attracts his ideal clients, and has gradually built a thriving Brand Art.

Here are some tips to help you successfully communicate your niche market.

Conveying Your Niche Market Through Your Digital Footprint:
To effectively communicate your niche market, it is essential to ensure that your website, portfolio, and marketing materials consistently convey the types of photography you specialise in and the category of clients you serve. Your branding, imagery, and messaging should be designed with your target market in mind, creating a cohesive and compelling representation of your niche. By clearly expressing your area of expertise,

you can attract customers who are specifically seeking the services you offer and differentiate yourself from photographers with a broader focus.

Highlighting Your Specialisation and Connecting with Your Audience:

Your website serves as a powerful tool to showcase your areas of specialisation and unique value proposition. Through carefully selected and curated photographs that resonate with your target audience, you can create an immediate connection and captivate their attention. Additionally, provide information on your website that addresses the specific needs and concerns of the demographic you are targeting. By illustrating a deep understanding of their challenges and desires, you establish credibility and build trust. Furthermore, a strong portfolio that features your best work in your niche will enhance your chances of attracting clients who appreciate your mission and artistic style, reinforcing your positioning in the market.

Amplifying Your Reach:

Whilst your website is a critical component of your online presence, it's important to extend your marketing efforts beyond your website. Use a variety of channels, including social media platforms, email marketing, and other advertising channels, to connect with and engage your niche audience. Craft compelling messages and content that resonates with your target demographic, while focusing on their specific interests and preferences. Make sure that the messaging and visual style of all your marketing materials are consistent with your brand identity. By diversifying your marketing channels and tailoring your content, you can expand your reach and connect with a broader audience within your niche.

Showcasing Expertise in Client Interactions:

Your interactions with clients provide an opportunity to showcase your expertise and reinforce your value proposition. During consultations and discussions, make a conscious effort to highlight the benefits of your specialised services. Convey an in-depth awareness of their pain points and needs, and how your offerings directly address those requirements. You can customise your approach and show that you can deliver tailored solutions by actively listening to and interacting with customers. This personalised attention and expertise will not only instill confidence in clients but also differentiate you as a photographer who truly understands their unique requirements.

SUMMARY:

FROM FART TO ART

Brand Fart

Lack of clarity in your niche market communication can lead to misunderstandings and missed opportunities. If your branding, messaging, and interactions don't reflect your specialisation, potential clients might have trouble comprehending what makes you distinguishable from other photographers or what unique value you can offer.

Brand Art

Effectively communicating your niche market involves expressing your specialisation through your website and portfolio, tailoring your marketing materials to your target audience, amplifying your reach through various channels, and showcasing your expertise in client interactions. By consistently conveying your niche, you can attract the right clients, establish a strong brand presence, and position yourself as a trusted and sought-after photographer within your designated professional field.

FART/5:

Not Positioning Your Brand to Stand Out

You strive as a photographer to stand out from the competition and attract your ideal clients by showcasing your unique abilities, style, and vision. However, it can be challenging to make a name for yourself in the saturated photography industry. The solution lies in strategically positioning your brand in a way that sets it apart from the rest and appeals to your target audience.

Dy cleverly positioning your brand, you can express your value proposition and competitive advantage while catering to the needs and preferences of your intended demographic. Being distinctive will make you more memorable, visible, and reputable as a brand, which will ultimately result in more bookings, higher rates, and a more sustainable business.

In an oversupplied marketplace, where photographers abound, the success story of Brandon Woelfel highlights the importance of mastering the art of making an industry imprint to create a unique and unforgettable presence in the business of photography.

Niching, and niching down, was one of the first steps Brandon took to position his brand. Rather than trying to be relevant to a broad clientele as a traditional portrait photographer, he identified a specific aesthetic and theme that resonated with him and spoke to his artistic sensibilities. His signature storytelling style, characterised by whimsical atmospheres and magical editing, became the cornerstone of his brand.

To further solidify his brand positioning, Brandon took his niche specialisation to the next level. He understood the power of becoming extremely targeted while expanding his customised services to attract new clients. By focusing on an isolated segment within his area of expertise, singular female portraits surrounded by dramatic lighting, he created a distinct sub-niche within his already narrow genre. This allowed him to establish himself as an authority and become the go-to choice for those craving that particular discipline of photography.

Additionally, Brandon acknowledged the value of pinpointing market gaps in order to effectively strengthen his brand. He observed the prevailing trends in photography and sought to offer something different and refreshing. By identifying areas where his unique aesthetic could fill a void and staying attuned to the evolving needs and desires of the market, he was able to position his brand as a solution to their unmet demands. With this calculated approach, he was able to seize untapped opportunities and assert himself as an influential pioneer.

Brandon focused on giving his customers an unrivalled experience on top of providing his distinctive photography style. Beyond the final images, he created an atmosphere of wonder and enchantment during his sessions, engaging his subjects and bringing his artistic vision to life. Going beyond traditional photoshoots, and offering an immersive and memorable experience, helped elevate Brandon's Brand Art and establish long-lasting relationships with his clients.

Brandon Woelfel's success as a photographer is testament to the power of strategic brand positioning. Taking inspiration from Brandon's strategies, we learn the importance of niching down, recognising market gaps, and offering a tailored experience to a specific demographic. By doing so, he has positioned his brand as an authority, captured the attention of his audience, and subsequently achieved sustained prosperity in a competitive industry.

Here are some strategies to help you successfully position your brand.

Niche it Down:

To stay relevant and dynamic after identifying your niche, it is vital to constantly improve and adapt it. By niching down again, you can develop a unique Brand Art that addresses your ideal client directly and establishes your authority in that sector. If you specialise in pet photography, for instance, you could further define your niche by photographing only dogs. This would allow you to craft a targeted marketing plan and position yourself as the go-to expert for dog owners.

Niching it Down Again:

Niching down even further can help you become highly specialised whilst broadening your customised offerings to draw in new customers. Using the same pet photography example, you could focus on shooting only a specific breed of dog, like the French Bulldog. By narrowing your focus once more, you position your photography business to stand out and reinforce your position as an authority in that specific sub-niche.

Identify Gaps in the Market:

Look for areas of photography where there is a gap in the market. This might be a particular kind of photography that isn't provided by other photographers in your field, or a popular style that isn't being executed as individuals would like. By identifying gaps in the market, you can position your brand to fill the void and establish a competitive advantage.

Focus on a Specific Demographic:

Focusing on a demographic category, such as age, sex, or ethnicity, can help you tailor your photography services to meet the specific needs and preferences of that particular segment. For instance, a photographer might decide to focus on capturing the beauty of senior women by showcasing their grace and wisdom in stunning portraits. By concentrating on an exclusive group of people, you can hone your abilities, create a notable aesthetic, and establish yourself as a specialist in that area.

Leverage Indoor or Outdoor Lighting:

The choice of lighting plays a key role in how photographers position their brand. Choosing indoor or studio shooting offers a controlled environment that enables precise light manipulation to create the desired atmosphere and style, consistent with the identity of your brand. It signifies professionalism and attention to detail, which might align with photographers seeking a curated, polished look. On the other hand, shooting outdoors with natural light infuses authenticity and a sense of connection with the surrounding environment. It's perfect for photographers who want to show off a more organic, natural side. Both approaches have their advantages and can be leveraged strategically to enhance your brand's distinctiveness and resonate with your target audience. The decision ultimately hinges on your photographic discipline and the brand image you aim to convey.

Offer a Unique Experience:

By giving your clientele a special and memorable experience, you differentiate yourself from the competition and build a solid reputation as a top photographer in your niche. Offering extra services like hair and makeup, unique props, or location scouting could be one way to further customise and cater the shoot to the client's requirements. By providing an unforgettable experience, you can position your brand as one that goes above and beyond for its customers, and establish a reputation for offering first-rate service.

FROM FART TO ART

Brand Fart

Making the mistake of not properly positioning your brand to stand out within its intended market is a potentially catastrophic oversight. Your photography business runs the risk of being perceived as average and unremarkable if you provide a mediocre or uninspired experience and fail to define your niche, pay attention to market gaps, target a particular demographic, and strategically leverage lighting. As a result, it may be challenging to distinguish your business from competitors' services and attract new clients whilst retaining existing ones.

Brand Art

To succeed as a photographer, it's important to differentiate yourself from the competition by positioning your brand in a way that appeals to your intended demographic. By niching down, identifying gaps in the market and choosing the right lighting environment, you can establish yourself as an expert in your specific sector and offer an exclusive experience to your clients.

FART/6:

Not Offering Unique and High-Value Services for Your Niche Market

It is insufficient for a photographer to merely provide all-inclusive, generic Brand Fart services to appeal to everyone. You can differentiate yourself from the competition and establish yourself as an authority in your field by concentrating on your niche market and offering unique, high-value services that address their specific needs and desires.

But how do you identify these special services, and what makes them valuable to your clients? Here are some tips.

Perform Market Research:

Performing market research is a crucial step in offering unique and high-value services to your niche. It involves diving deep into understanding the requirements, preferences, and expectations of your target audience. By investing time and effort into researching your market, you can gain valuable insights that will guide you in creating services that truly resonate with your clients.

Start by identifying the qualities and attributes that your ideal demographic seeks in a photographer. Are they looking for someone who specialises in a specific style or genre? Do they value creativity, attention to detail, or a unique artistic approach? Understanding these desired qualities will help you shape your services to meet their criteria.

Additionally, it's essential to grasp the type of experience your target market is hoping for. Are they seeking a fun and relaxed atmosphere during the photo session? Do they want a personalised and customised approach that caters to their individual preferences? Understanding their desired photoshoot will allow you to design services that align with their priorities and create a memorable and enjoyable environment for your clients.

Brainstorm Creative Ideas:

Your target market is probably seeking something different from standard photography services. Don't be afraid to think outside the box and provide them with one-of-a-kind, cutting-edge services that they can only get from you. If you specialise in social media content photography, for instance, you might offer a "Social Media Influencer Package" that includes a creative photo session capturing unique and eye-catching visuals tailored for social media platforms.

This package could also include additional services such as content editing, caption writing assistance, a personalised content calendar, or strategic advice on maximising engagement and reach on different social media channels. By providing a comprehensive package specifically designed for social media influencers, you can help them elevate their online presence, attract more followers, and stand out in the crowded digital landscape.

Listen to Your Clients:

Pay close attention to the suggestions and criticisms of your clients. What aspects of your work do they enjoy? What could you improve? This will give you a clear understanding of what your clients want and value in a photographer. Using the social media content photographer example, listening to clients could mean paying attention to the types of material they get the most interactions or shares on their social media channels. By analysing their audience's preferences and engagement metrics, you can identify the types of visuals, themes, and styles that resonate with their target market.

This could include experimenting with different types of posts such as before-and-after photo series or time-lapse videos, behind-the-scenes shots, user-generated content, or interactive polls and quizzes. By actively listening to your clients' feedback and monitoring the performance of their social media content, you can continually refine and optimise your photography services to meet their specific goals and drive greater audience participation.

Examine the Competition:
To position yourself effectively in the market, it's crucial to thoroughly examine the competition. Take the time to research and analyse the pricing structures, websites, and body of work of other photographers operating in your specific area of expertise. By doing so, you can gain valuable insights into their strengths, advantages, and unique selling points that set them apart. This examination serves as a valuable benchmark to identify areas where you can differentiate yourself and create a unique competitive advantage in the services you offer.

Once you have identified the potential clients for your business, you can build a Brand Art that truly appeals to your target market by understanding the requirements and preferences of your niche. Your intended audience will be able to tell your brand apart from your competitors by the services you provide them that meet their needs.

Remember, it is extremely important to communicate the value of the specialised services you offer to them. Be sure to justify the expense of your photographic packages by elaborating thoroughly on the benefits they provide. By offering services that are inventive and of high value, you will be able to distinguish your Brand Art as an authority in your field and command higher rates for your work.

FROM FART TO ART

Brand Fart

If you don't offer your target audience anything unique or valuable through your photography services, you risk being perceived as a basic photographer. It may be challenging to differentiate yourself from the competition and attract high-paying clients if you don't engage in research, exercise creative thinking, and pursue innovative ideas.

Brand Art

If you want to stand out as a photographer, you must provide your niche market with personalised and highly valuable services. To establish yourself as a specialist in your field, carry out extensive research, listen to your clients, and produce creative and one-of-a-kind services. You'll be able to charge more for your packages as a result, and gain a key advantage over your competition.

BRAND FART MESSAGING

⌐ ¬
L ⌐

Crafting a compelling brand message is essential for photographers who want to distance themselves from industry competitors. Your brand message communicates to your target market your business's values, vision, and primary point of differentiation. It distinguishes you from your creative rivals and appeals to your ideal clients. Unfortunately, a lot of photographers have trouble creating a strategy for their brand messaging and end up making Brand Fart misjudgments that hurt their reputation.

For me, as a boudoir photographer, my journey began with a passion for capturing the natural beauty and femininity of the female form. Given the saturation of this niche market, I knew that honing a distinctive visual aesthetic was crucial to developing a narrative that would distinguish me.

During the height of the 2020 pandemic, while watching musician Maxwell's "This Woman's Work" music video, a particular scene caught my eye. The atmosphere was sultry, seductive, and unforgettably memorable due to the rich green cinematic colouration. I was confident I had found the inspiration I needed to create a signature look that would set me apart.

Using green tones as the foundation, complemented with orange and yellow hues, I developed a distinct colour palette that gives my work a unique and identifiable ambience. I also made the conscious decision to photograph my models in low-light scenery, which heightens the intimacy and sensuality of my images. Additionally, by incorporating lighting props or window shades to create a light source within my photoshoot set-ups, I was able to capture the sensuous intensity and raw emotion of my subjects in a way that is both captivating and visually striking.

This specific photographic and editing approach has grown to be a fundamental component of my brand messaging as it reflects the mood and feeling I want to evoke in my audience. It distinguishes me from other photographers and enables me to produce a body of work that is cohesive and instantly recognisable as being mine.

However, I didn't truly find my voice in the industry until I discovered my speciality in photography for lingerie brands. By combining my love for capturing the human form's natural beauty with my interest in lingerie fashion, working with these boutique brands has allowed me to produce images that not only showcase the lingerie but also empower the women who are wearing it. I use my photographic abilities to address the essence of the idea that every woman deserves to feel beautiful, confident, and at home in their skin.

My brand message centres around creating a safe and welcoming space for women to express themselves, celebrate their bodies and their unique qualities, and feel liberated and self-assured. Through my photography, I hope to inspire women to love themselves and embrace their individuality, while also highlighting the beauty and quality of the lingerie brands I work with.

Understanding your target market, outlining your brand's core values, and crafting an aesthetic that emphasises your expertise in the field and appeals to your ideal clients are all necessary steps in developing an effective brand message. By avoiding common Brand Fart missteps and clearly articulating your brand message across a range of marketing channels, you can develop brand recognition and cement your authority in the industry.

In this chapter, we'll explore various strategies for establishing an effective brand narrative that resonates with your target audience. We'll provide you with useful pointers and tools to help you create a Brand Art story that stands out and attracts the clients you desire. By constructing a powerful brand message, you can differentiate yourself in the photography industry and build a thriving business.

FART/7:

Failing to Craft a Distinctive Brand Message Through Your Editing Style

Your distinctive editing style serves as the cornerstone of your brand message as a photographer. It's the distinguishing characteristic that sets you apart from other photographers and establishes your Brand Art. A unique editing approach is not just about making your photos look aesthetically pleasing, it is also about creating a consistent and recognisable look and feel that represents your brand identity.

Your photo manipulation technique is how you alter images to produce a particular appearance or mood. It can be bold and dramatic or soft and enchanting. It may be colourful and saturated or subdued and desaturated.

Whatever your preferred look, it must be recognisable as your visual trademark.

Photographers need to avoid the Brand Fart of failing to create a distinctive brand message through their editing appearance for the reasons below.

Communicates Your Uniqueness:
In today's competitive photography industry, it's essential to stand out from the crowd and offer something unique to potential clients. An original editing style can help you differentiate yourself from other photographers in your market and create a signature look that becomes your artistic tag. By developing your aesthetic, you create a visual language that distinguishes your work and helps you attract clients who appreciate your vision.

Relays Your Brand Vision and Values:
Your design style isn't just about the technical aspects of editing, it's an extension of your values as a photographer, as well as your personality and your photographic perspective. Your image enhancement technique has the power to evoke emotions, set the mood, and communicate a distinct sense of taste, and it should align with your overall brand message. For instance, if your brand narrative is all about capturing your subjects' unfiltered states of mind, your editing style could reflect that by using a minimalistic approach with desaturated colours and natural lighting.

Builds Consistency and Trust:

Consistency is the key to building a successful photography brand. A unique editing personality helps you establish a consistent and recognisable look across all of your photographs, making it easy for your audience to identify your art. Coherence in your retouching method also allows clients to have trust in your work, as they know what to expect from your services and they will have confidence that you can deliver the same level of quality for them. As a result, they will be more inclined to refer others to your brand, bringing in more customers and creating a positive feedback loop.

Creates a Memorable Experience:

A distinctive editing approach improves the overall client experience. Long after the photoshoot is over, your customers will remember their interaction with your brand if your post-processing style is recognisable and consistent. Your clients will feel a connection to you emotionally as a result of this association between your photo-altering style and their memories, which will keep them using your services for many years to come.

Experimenting with Editing Techniques and Software Programs

The process of developing a distinctive editing aesthetic takes time and experimentation. While there is no universal system for creating a personal retouching style, here are some actionable tips that can help you along the way.

Explore Editing Techniques:
The post-production stage of photography offers endless possibilities for enhancing the mood and visual impact of your images. By venturing into different editing methods, you can unlock the full potential of your photographs and produce a distinct style that resonates with your artistic vision. You can experiment with different adjustments and techniques to manipulate key elements of your images, such as contrast, brightness, and saturation levels, giving them a distinctive and alluring appearance.

Manipulating contrast can drastically alter the photo's feel, with increased contrast yielding bold and dynamic images, while decreased contrast creates a softer, ethereal ambience. Adjusting brightness influences mood, increasing it for vibrancy or reducing it for mystery. Saturation controls colour intensity, with higher saturation producing vivid visuals and lower saturation evoking nostalgia or elegance. Trying out different combinations of these methods can help you find the ideal harmony for your artistic voice.

Additionally, exploring various colour-grading techniques can add an extra layer of creativity to your editing process. By manipulating the hues and tones in your images, colour grading enables you to create a recognisable and harmonious colour palette. Try using warm colours to evoke a cosy atmosphere or cool colours to convey a serene vibe. By playing with different colour grading techniques, you can refine your style and create a visual language that is uniquely yours.

Broaden Your Creative Toolkit:
Broadening your creative toolkit involves exploring different software applications for editing. Each program offers unique tools and capabilities that can significantly impact the outcome of your photographs. By experimenting with multiple programs, you can discover the one that aligns best with your brand narrative. Some software applications may provide advanced retouching options, while others excel in special effects or intuitive user interfaces.

To maximise your creative potential and improve your post-production workflow, it's crucial to devote time to learning and mastering various software options, like Adobe Lightroom and Photoshop, and Capture One. Remember, finding the right editing software is like finding the perfect brush for a painter; it enhances your skills and allows you to express your creativity more effectively.

Borrow Techniques:
Drawing inspiration from other photographers and artists can be a valuable source for sharpening your editing

skills. Take the time to analyse the work of creatives whose post-processing approaches you respect. To discover what makes them unique, pay close attention to their techniques, compositions, and overall aesthetic. While it's perfectly acceptable to borrow ideas and concepts from these sources, it's essential to infuse your own individuality and personal touch into the process.

Try incorporating these borrowed methods into your workflow, then modify them to fit your particular preferences and vision. By doing so, you can produce a distinctive editing approach that reflects your artistic voice and resonates with your audience. Never forget that the idea is to learn and develop from the inspirations around you to create your own unique and compelling photo enhancement style. Utilise the power of borrowing and cross-pollination within the creative community and let the work of others inspire you to reach new heights of your creative expression.

Developing a personal editing aesthetic is a continuous journey that evolves with time. Take advantage of the opportunity to experiment, explore new techniques, and perfect your style to align with your professional development as a Brand Art photographer. It's important to remember that the process of exploring image-altering techniques is not solely technical, it's about unleashing your imagination and finding methods that connect with your photographic vision. Take the time to play with different adjustments, analyse their impact, and cultivate a refined editing workflow that truly showcases what makes you special. Allow the process to become a means of self-expression, breathing life into your photographs and capturing the essence of your artistic voice. Embrace the evolution of your photo-modifying journey and let it be a reflection of your creative growth and passion.

FROM FART TO ART

Brand Fart

Photographers who adopt a generic and uninspired post-processing style undermine their brand message, which can have detrimental consequences. Without a distinctive editing aesthetic, inconsistencies and a lack of trust can arise with your audience, causing you to fade into the sea of competitors, compromise the communication of your brand's vision and values, and you will ultimately deliver an underwhelming experience for your clients.

Brand Art

A unique editing style is essential for creating a strong photography brand. It allows you to differentiate yourself from competitors, communicate your brand philosophy and artistic viewpoint, build consistency and trust, and create a memorable experience for your clients. Spend time developing your photo-altering method and remember that it's not just about learning the technical aspects of manipulating images, it creates a visual trademark that becomes the foundation of your overall brand message.

FART/8:

Overcomplicating Your Brand Story

The lifeblood of your photography business is your brand story. It helps you connect with your audience and distinguishes you from your competitors. A carefully crafted brand story can foster relationships, establish trust, and ultimately promote business growth.

Here we'll discuss what a brand story is, why it's significant, and how to avoid the common Brand Fart errors that photographers make when developing their own.

What is a Brand Story?

A brand story is fundamentally a narrative that outlines the history of your photography business. It conveys your identity, your values, and what makes you different. Your brand story ought to capture the essence of your business in a way that appeals to your ideal audience.

Why is a Brand Story Important?

Your brand story is essential because it gives you a competitive edge and gains the audience's trust. It communicates your moral principles and worldview, which can help you connect emotionally with your clients and establish a long-lasting relationship with them.

One of the biggest Brand Farts that photographers commit when crafting their brand story is overcomplicating it. When your story is overly complex, you risk losing your audience's interest and sounding artificial or fake. It's crucial to concentrate on authenticity and simplicity to prevent this. Without any unessential information or jargon, your brand story should be a concise and clear representation of who you are and what you have to offer.

The failure to make their photography story relevant to their target market is another Brand Fart made by photographers. The value that you bring to your niche and the issues you are resolving for your audience should be highlighted in your brand narrative. You'll discover that your story resonates on a personal level and separates you from the competition when it is narrowly focused on your field of interest.

An excellent example of a photographer who has effectively leveraged their personal story into their branding is sought-after photographer and creative director Mat Abad, also known as Badboi.

He was raised in the Philippines' slums before relocating to Los Angeles in his early teens and pursuing a career as a professional dancer. His life course was altered for good when his friend secretly submitted his photographic work to agencies, launching his career as a photographer.

At first, Badboi's work centred on street photography, which sought to highlight the energy and vitality of the city. Nevertheless, over time he began to incorporate his love of Hip-Hop culture into his work, producing highly stylised, vibrant photos that frequently featured iconic figures. As an outdoor portrait photographer who now spends his time snapping some of the best models in the world in beautiful natural settings, Badboi's work has a unique Californian soul vibe.

The central theme of Badboi's brand narrative is his rise from modest beginnings to prominent statuo ao a creative director and photographer. His distinctive photography style, which he describes as a fusion of street culture, pop art, and fashion, has served as the foundation of his brand story. Due to his unique aesthetic, he has been able to stand out in the marketplace and draw in prestigious clients like Adidas, Puma, and Timberland.

Create Your Brand Story

You must concentrate on four essential components when creating your brand story.

Simplicity:
When crafting your brand story, it is crucial to prioritise simplicity. Your story should be clear, concise, and easily comprehensible, enabling your audience to grasp its essence and message without any confusion. By avoiding jargon or complex technical terms that might alienate or confuse your market, you ensure that your story remains accessible and relatable to a wider range of individuals. Presenting your narrative in a straightforward and easily digestible manner, you can effectively communicate the principles that make up your brand and connect with your ideal client on a more intimate level.

Authenticity:
When crafting your brand story, it is important to embrace authenticity as a guiding principle. Your story should genuinely reflect your unique identity, principles, and beliefs. By staying true to yourself and showcasing vulnerability, you establish trust with your market. Once

your audience perceives your realness, they are more likely to connect with you on an even greater scale, as they resonate with your sincere voice and narrative. Sharing your experiences, perspectives, and journey with the public in a transparent manner helps to build a relationship of trust and loyalty that can help you stand out in a saturated marketplace.

Relevance:

When crafting your brand story, it is essential to ensure its relevance to your niche market. Your story should be in line with your target audience's particular needs, interests, and aspirations. By understanding their desires and challenges, you can tailor your narrative to address those pain points and highlight the distinct value that you bring to the table. Communicating how your unique offerings and expertise directly benefit your chosen demographic creates a compelling message that resonates with them. You position yourself as the ideal solution and build a strong bond with your target market by emphasising the relevance of your brand story to their lives and highlighting the precise ways you can meet their needs.

Consistency:

Keeping your brand story consistent across all touchpoints is fundamental for creating a powerful and recognisable identity. It involves aligning your messaging, visual elements, and overall tone of communication across platforms such as your website, social media profiles, and marketing materials. A sense of cohesion that reinforces your narrative and values in the minds of your market is created by maintaining a consistent brand experience. Consistency builds trust and familiarity, allowing your audience to develop a deeper connection with your brand. It also strengthens your business's reputation, as a harmonious message and background showcase reliability and professionalism. Whether it's the language you use, the imagery you share, or the way you engage with your target demographic, maintaining consistency throughout your brand channels helps you leave a lasting impression and build meaningful relationships with your audience.

Testing and Refining Your Brand Story

It's vital that you test and refine your brand story after you've created it. Get feedback from a focus group, or close friends and family, by narrating your photography journey. Utilise this constructive criticism to improve your message and make it more engaging and memorable. Furthermore, it's crucial to regularly evaluate your story to make sure that it still reflects your current identity, values, and beliefs.

Keep in mind that building your brand story is a continuous process, not a single event. As your photography business evolves, so should the message behind your brand. By persistently enhancing and reinforcing your brand narrative, you can develop a powerful photography Brand Art that is distinguishable in your specific market and helps you differentiate yourself from other photographers.

SUMMARY:

FROM FART TO ART

Brand Fart

A common branding error that can harm your photography business is overcomplicating your brand story. You may lose potential clients if your brand narrative is unclear, irrelevant, or inconsistent, as they won't know what you stand for or why they should choose you over other photographers.

Brand Art

For your photography business, creating a compelling brand story that connects with your target demographic can be transformative. You can build a strong brand identity that sets you apart from the competition and engages your audience emotionally by keeping it straightforward, genuine, relevant, and consistent. With the right brand narrative, you can create a profitable photography company that endures the test of time.

FART/9:

Failing to Build an Emotional Connection with Your Audience

As a photographer, you might become preoccupied with honing your technical abilities and getting the ideal shot. However, you must recognise the significance of emotions and how they are essential to connecting with your audience if you want to create a successful Brand Art. Many photographers make the error of concentrating solely on their skills and photographic methods without taking into account the potential sentimental impact of their work and the message it can convey. This may rooult in a flat, uninspired Brand Fart that struggles to differentiate itself in a competitive market.

Using a variety of avenues, Badboi is a perfect illustration of a photographer who has successfully forged a special bond with his audience. To begin with, he uses storytelling in his photography to engage viewers emotionally. Badboi captures a sense of youth and freedom that resonates with his market by presenting a visual narrative through his images, which frequently feature young and beautiful models in natural scenery. This method has helped him establish a deep connection with those he inspires and craft a distinctive personal brand.

Additionally, Badboi has been able to create a sentimental attachment with his audience thanks to his notable aesthetic and artistic approach to photography. His use of vibrant colours, natural lighting, and unconventional angles have helped him create a signature look that sets him apart from other photographers. His visual style has drawn a specific audience that connects with his vision, and by producing high-quality work that is consistent with his brand, he has been able to establish a close relationship with his market, notably his 500K+ Instagram followers.

The connection Badboi has with his audience is also a result of his core values and principles. He is passionate about social justice and has used his platform to advocate for important world issues. His charitable organisation, Karmagawa, has supported several initiatives, including the provision of clean water, educational programmes, and support for endangered species. By integrating his brand with values that his followers care about, Badboi has been able to gain their trust and loyalty.

Drawing inspiration from Badboi's accomplishments, photographers can gain insight into how to construct an emotional bond with their audience that goes beyond their work. By employing visual storytelling, developing a unique style, and aligning your brand with your values, you can connect with your market on a personal level and build a devoted following.

Strategies to Engage Your Audience Emotionally

How can you avoid making the mistake of failing to engage your audience emotionally? Here are some strategies you can implement.

Craft a Compelling Visual Story:

Crafting a photographic narrative is an indispensable skill for photographers as it enables them to effectively convey their unique perspectives and tell captivating storioo through their images. A visual story goes beyond being a mere collection of photographs; it is a meticulously curated body of work that takes the viewer on a compelling journey, evokes emotions, and forges connections. Through careful selection and organisation of the various design components within a frame, photographers can produce a powerful narrative that invites the audience to immerse themselves and interpret the scene in their own personal way.

The arrangement of these elements plays a key role in creating a visually appealing and effective composition. You can make deliberate choices about where to place each component within the frame to guide the viewer's attention, create a sense of balance or imbalance, convey a specific mood or statement, and enhance the overall storytelling impact of the image.

To make a composition more dynamic, you could, for instance, use the rule of thirds to place the main subject off-centre. You could utilise leading lines to guide the viewer's gaze through the frame or include a strong foreground element to add depth and dimension. The arrangement of colours and contrasts can also evoke strong emotions or emphasise specific features within the image.

Photographers who have the ability to construct a visual narrative possess an influential tool for communicating their style, vision, and mission. This talent plays a pivotal role in building a strong Brand Art and fostering a dedicated following. By skillfully weaving together images that convey a cohesive story, you can showcase your unique artistic voice, and leave an unforgettable impression on audiences who resonate with your work.

A well-crafted visual message has the power to elevate the value and impact of a photographer's portfolio. By harnessing the Brand Art of storytelling through your images, you can stand out in a highly competitive industry and create a profound and memorable impression on viewers. Through the mastery of visual storytelling, you can cultivate a distinct identity that captures the imagination of your ideal client, opens doors to new opportunities, and propels your career forward.

Use Visual Elements to Evoke Emotions:
Visual elements are a crucial part of your brand. All of these components, from your logo and colour scheme to your website design and marketing materials, should be carefully created to stimulate the appropriate emotions in your target audience. The psychology of colour, typography, and other design features can all be used to your advantage to evoke strong feelings in your audience.

Share Social Issues Close to Your Heart:
Photographers have the power to forge a deep emotional bond with their audience by sharing issues that hold personal significance. When you actively participate in philanthropic activities like volunteering at a local church, providing assistance to the homeless,

or empowering underprivileged youth with new skills, you exemplify your unwavering dedication to making a positive impact.

It is essential, however, that you approach these endeavours sincerely, with no ulterior motive of manipulating your audience. Genuine sharing of these experiences should stem from a heartfelt desire to raise awareness, inspire others, and contribute to meaningful change. Through this authentic engagement, photographers not only strengthen their Brand Art but also establish an intimate connection with their audience based on shared values and a collective commitment to improving the world.

SUMMARY:

FROM FART TO ART

Brand Fart

Neglecting emotional impact and focusing solely on technical skills can result in a lacklustre and unengaging brand that struggles to stand out in a competitive market. Without incorporating visual storytelling and authentic values into your brand strategy, you'll struggle to capture the hearts and minds of potential clients and will be in danger of becoming overshadowed by your peers who effectively engage their audience on a deeper, sentimental level.

Brand Art

Understanding the influence of emotions and the importance of establishing an intimate bond with your target demographic is essential to developing a strong photography brand message. Through the skillful use of storytelling in your images, you can engage viewers, create a lasting impression, and cultivate a devoted following that sincerely values and connects with your work. Additionally, by genuinely sharing your involvement in causes that truly resonate with your heart, you not only reinforce your personal brand but also form a profoundly touching relationship with your audience.

FART/10:

Choosing Not to Put Your Personality on Display

Photography is an intimate business, and your personality plays a pivotal role in forging a solid bond with your ideal market. It serves as a vital element in your Brand Art messaging, distinguishing you from other creative professionals in your field, and giving you a sense of individuality. By authentically presenting who you are, clients can personally connect with you, fostering a sense of comfort and confidence in their decision to hire your services.

People do business with people they like, and your audience wants to know who you are as a person, not just as a photographer. Incorporating your personality into your branding and marketing efforts can humanise your business and allow you to interact with your market demographic on a more intimate level.

Implementing Your Personality into Your Branding

There are many ways to integrate your personality into your branding. Here are some tips to get you started.

Develop a Brand Voice that Reflects Your Personality:

Your brand voice is how you communicate with your audience through your written and spoken words. Whether it's witty, informative, or sincere, develop a voice that best expresses your personality. Apply this tone consistently throughout all of your marketing channels, such as your website, social media accounts, video marketing, and emails.

Incorporate Personal Stories into Your Marketing:

Telling stories about your life, your experiences, and your passions will humanise your brand and increase its relatability. Do you love to go scouting for potential shoot locations? Do you enjoy experimenting with new photography gear? Share your process, results, and adventures with your audience. By giving your viewers a glimpse into your life and sharing your interests and hobbies, you give potential clients a peek behind the curtain and showcase what makes you tick as a person.

Additionally, don't be afraid to be transparent and share the unpolished side of your story. For instance, use social media networks to discuss the failures and setbacks you've experienced behind any success. Audiences find this content real and inspirational. Sharing your journey illustrates that you are more than just a photographer, you are a person with a distinct viewpoint and a compelling story.

Inject Humour into Your Marketing:

Introducing humour into your marketing can be a powerful tool for photographers looking to stand out in a saturated market. If you have a quirky character or personality for example, consider injecting it into your marketing. Laughter is a universal language that serves to unite people across different backgrounds and cultures, making it an effective way to build a bond with prospective clients. It can also create a more lighthearted and fun atmosphere, which can help put customers at ease and make them more comfortable working with you. But it's important to keep in mind that not all playful behaviour is appropriate for all audiences or circumstances. It's crucial to strike a balance between humour and professionalism to avoid offending or alienating potential clients.

Display Photos of Yourself:

Using photos of yourself on your website and marketing material can help to highlight your personality.

Select images that reflect your character and photographic aesthetic. Visitors are more likely to choose you over a generic or impersonal photographer when they can relate to and see the person behind the camera.

Be yourself:
The most important thing you can do to showcase your personality is to be yourself. When you present your unique traits, you are being your vulnerable self, and authenticity is key to establishing a genuine rapport with your target demographic. So don't try to be someone you're not. If you try to hide who you are, your audience will be able to tell if you're not being real, which can hurt your brand in the long run.

Benefits of Putting Your Personality on Display

There are several benefits to showcasing your personality in your branding efforts.

Engagement:
Showing off your personality allows you to establish a closer bond with your audience, which may result in higher levels of engagement. When people connect with a brand, they are more likely to interact with it.

Loyalty:

You can develop a devoted clientele who adore both your brand and your personality by showcasing who you are. This can lead to repeat business and referrals.

Differentiation:

In a competitive market, presenting your personality can help you differentiate yourself from the competition. Your personality is unique, and it is what makes your personal brand distinguishable.

Trust:

By displaying your personality, you establish your brand's reputation as genuine and approachable. Being comfortable expressing your personality can assist in developing the kind of brand trust that consumers seek out when making hiring decisions.

Confidence is attractive and contagious. When you are confident in your personality and brand, your clients will be more confident in you as well. By showing your personality, you are indicating that you are at ease with who you are and that you are a competent photographer. When attempting to win over potential customers, this can be a siqnificant selling point.

Keep in mind, no matter how hard you try, there will always be people who do not like your work or who you are as a person. Rejection is inevitable, it's just part of the game. However, it's not your job to be liked, it's your job to be yourself. It's fundamental that you remain true to what makes you human and not let individual opinions prevent you from expressing your aesthetic self. People who are truly for you will gravitate towards you, and the right clients will value you for being your real self.

Photographers, like any other creative professional, should never be afraid to show off their personalities, but it's also crucial to remember that displaying your personality doesn't mean you have to share every aspect of who you are and your life. Be mindful of what you share online and how it aligns with your audience and your overall brand messaging. Authenticity and relatability are things you should strive for, but professionalism should also be a priority.

FROM FART TO ART

Brand Fart

Photographers who are afraid to showcase their personalities may find themselves inadvertently creating a negative brand image. Consumers in today's market desire not only high-quality photography but also a relationship with the person behind the lens. By hiding your true self and conforming to industry norms, you will ultimately blend in with the crowd and lose potential clients who are looking to hire based on a personal bond.

Brand Art

Presenting your personality is an essential component of personal branding for photographers. It humanises your business, establishes a connection with your audience, and sets you apart from the competition. Incorporating your personality into your branding can be done in a variety of ways, including developing your brand voice, displaying photographs of yourself, incorporating personal stories, and introducing humour into your interactions and marketing.

FART/11:

Underestimating the Power of Word-of-Mouth and Referrals

Building your Brand Art as a photographer and reaching new clients can be a difficult task. However, word-of-mouth and referrals are two of your most effective marketing tools. In fact, according to research, up to 82% of new clientele for many photographers come from recommendations. So don't make the Brand Fart mistake of underestimating its power.

But why are recommendations and word-of-mouth so powerful? Simply put, trust. Someone is more likely to believe a recommendation about your services made by a family member, friend, or coworker, because they have faith in the source. This trust may attract new clients and raise the profile of your brand.

The advantages of recommendations and word-of-mouth are obvious. They can assist you in expanding your audience, establishing a solid brand, and boosting sales. Compared to other forms of marketing, referrals produce up to 16% more profit, which was highlighted in a recent survey. In your marketing plan, you must therefore give these strategies a top priority.

One photographer who has grown their photography business by utilising the influence of recommendations and word-of-mouth is Badboi. His referrals have been a powerful marketing tool because they come from trusted sources which carry more weight than traditional advertising methods.

The commercial achievements of Badboi can be attributed to his wide network of clients, who have helped him gain more exposure by introducing him to their business relationships. Additionally, collaborating with other creatives in the industry, such as models, stylists, and photographers, has allowed him to tap into their professional circles and attract new clients.

In addition to providing exceptional service, Badboi excels at cultivating a relaxed and enjoyable environment on set. His reputation for being easy to work with has helped him attract big-name clients and build a strong brand known for its quality and creativity.

As a photographer, following Badboi's example and focusing on building lasting relationships with clients and collaborators can help you establish a strong Brand Art and grow your business through the power of word-of-mouth and referrals.

Getting People to Talk About Your Brand

How can you get people to talk about your brand through referrals and word-of-mouth? Here are some pointers to get you going.

Provide Excellent Customer Service:
The secret to getting people to spread the word about your photography business is to give your customers excellent service. Surpass their expectations and provide a truly memorable experience by going above and beyond. Take the time to understand their needs, communicate effectively, and deliver exceptional results. Show genuine care and attention to detail in every interaction, ensuring that each customer feels valued and satisfied with their experience.

Ask For Referrals:
Don't be afraid to ask your satisfied customers for referrals. Reach out to them via email or make a personal phone call to thank them for their business and ask if they know of anyone who might need your services.

Explain the value of their recommendation and how it can help others discover your photography business. By actively seeking referrals, you open the door to new opportunities and expand your client base through trusted connections.

Offer Incentives:

For each new customer that a current client refers to you, you can reward them with a discount, a free photo session, or some financial incentive. This not only shows your appreciation for their support but also motivates your clients to promote your business further. The incentives create a win-win situation where both parties benefit. It encourages your satisfied customers to become brand advocates and actively refer your services to others.

Network With Other Professionals in Your Niche:

Attend events, join groups and online communities, and build relationships with other photographers and professionals in your niche. By connecting with like-minded individuals, you can tap into a network of potential referrals. Collaborate on projects, share insights, and support each other's creative businesses. When professionals in your industry know and trust your work, they are more likely to push clients in your direction when they need photography services that align with your expertise.

Encourage Positive Word-of-Mouth on Social Platforms:

Establish a strong presence on social media platforms where your target audience is active, and encourage past clients and followers to promote your brand by sharing your content and leaving positive comments. Engaging with their online reviews, remarks, and messages develops a sense of community and fosters new relationships with potential customers. Your active presence on social media creates opportunities for others to discover and talk about your photography brand, ultimately spurring business growth.

The power of word-of-mouth and referrals plays a vital role in a photographer's overall brand messaging. These tactics spread your brand message organically, reaching a wider audience who may be more inclined to trust the opinions of friends, family, or colleagues. Harnessing the influence of word-of-mouth and referrals not only strengthens your brand narrative and expands your client base, but also reinforces your Brand Art reputation, establishing you as a trusted and sought-after photographer in the industry.

FROM FART TO ART

Brand Fart

Underestimating the power of word-of-mouth and referrals can have disastrous consequences for a photography business. Neglecting client satisfaction, disregarding opportunities for customers to share your work, and undervaluing online engagement and reviews can lead to a weak and unsustainable brand that struggles to attract new business. Failing to recognise the importance of these marketing tactics and the implications they have on your brand messaging as a whole puts your company at risk of eventual failure.

Brand Art

Leveraging the power of word-of-mouth and referrals is crucial for any photography business to succeed. By consistently providing exceptional customer service, exceeding expectations, and nurturing positive relationships with clients, you can inspire them to become enthusiastic brand advocates who willingly share their positive experiences. These recommendations not only attract new clients but also spread your brand message, enhancing your reputation and visibility.

FART/12:

Neglecting to Test and Continuously Evolving Your Brand Message

As a photographer, it's fundamental that you build your Brand Art to differentiate yourself from competitors and draw in and retain clients. However, it's easy to fall into the Brand Fart trap of neglecting to test and continuously evolving your photography brand messaging. You may experience revenue decline, clientele loss and stagnation as a consequence.

To avoid this, start by realising that your brand message is not a fixed entity, but rather a living, breathing reflection of who you are, what you stand for, and why you are the best choice for your clients. To stay current with shifting consumer demands and market dynamics, it's essential to test and enhance your brand narrative from the outset.

Your brand message serves as the foundation for how you communicate your unique perspective and connect with your audience through your images. Continuous testing and evolution of your brand narrative will enable you to uncover what resonates with your target demographic, refine your storytelling methods, and stay relevant in a dynamic industry. Embracing change and adapting your brand message ensures that you remain compelling, engaging, and innovative, ultimately forging a stronger bond with your clientele and cementing your position as a creative force in the world of photography.

Gathering feedback through customer surveys, market research, and other data-driven insights is also a useful way to test and develop your Brand Art narrative. This can show you where you need to make changes and give you enlightening information about how to better serve your clients' needs.

Developing and evolving your brand messaging is crucial for establishing yourself as a leader in the photography industry. To stay ahead of the competition and maintain your position as a trusted authority, it's important to stay up-to-date with the latest trends and technologies in the field. Keeping a pulse on industry advancements, you can effectively integrate them into your brand narrative to highlight your expertise and innovation. This indicates to your clients that you are at the forefront of your market, constantly evolving and adapting to meet their expectations. By aligning your brand message with current trends and technologies, you can position yourself as a go-to photographer for innovative solutions and services, further solidifying your reputation as a figurehead in your area of specialisation.

Keep in mind that your brand narrative is dynamic and ever-evolving. Small, gradual changes periodically have a greater impact than large, abrupt changes. Through email newsletters, social media updates, and other forms of outreach, you can keep your customers informed and interested in your brand while strengthening your relationship with them. You will ultimately stay ahead of the curve, create Brand Art that connects with your target market, and maintain relevance, engagement, and competitiveness as time progresses by testing and continually improving your brand message.

SUMMARY:
FROM FART TO ART

Brand Fart

If you do not put the time and effort into testing and evolving your brand message, you may end up with a stale and out-of-date photography business that your target market cannot relate to. By neglecting to collect feedback, refining your visual storytelling, and keeping an eye on trends, your brand will be in danger of being unable to differentiate itself from the competition and becoming irrelevant in an increasingly competitive market.

Brand Art

Developing and testing your brand message is a key component of creating a successful photography business. You can establish how to evolve your brand narrative over time by creating a strategy for getting customer feedback, conducting market research, and keeping up with industry trends. Keep in mind that even small adjustments can have a significant impact on how people view your brand. You can make sure that your business message is relevant and continues to resonate with your target audience by remaining adaptable, flexible, and innovative.

BRAND FART PRICING

Setting the right price for your photography services is crucial to the success of your business. It can be a daunting task, especially if you are new to the industry. However, finding the perfect price point that strikes a balance between making a profit and remaining competitive is a challenge for many photographers.

At the start of my photography venture, I also found it difficult to set my prices. Like many other creatives, I experienced imposter syndrome, which made me question whether my work was worthy of being paid for. However, after charging a model £30 for a fashion shoot portfolio update a few months into my journey, I realised that I had crossed over from photography being a hobby to a potential career.

As I gained more experience and confidence, I came to understand the importance of pricing based on the value I offered individuals. Instead of just billing by the hour or for a predetermined package, I began to consider the particular requirements of each customer and the worth that my work would add to their business or personal life.

By employing this strategy, I was able to differentiate myself from my competitors and attract clients who valued my expertise and the calibre of my work. Eighteen months after my first paid job, I was commanding four figures as a freelance photographer for up to an 8-hour photoshoot.

Despite still being relatively new to the industry and getting paid my asking prices, I noticed that many photographers, some of whom had been in the industry for over a decade, were only managing to demand a few hundred pounds from their clients, irrespective of the outstanding quality of their work.

After some investigation, I realised that my photographer peers' knowledge of pricing was flawed. Instead of charging for value, quality, and niche, they were charging for time. They struggled to encourage repeat business from their clients and took on any job, regardless of whether it fit with their area of expertise.

In this chapter, we'll delve into the differences between Brand Fart and Brand Art in the realm of pricing. Additionally, we'll discuss the typical pricing errors that photographers make and offer workable solutions to prevent them. We'll also explore how to correctly price your services by taking into account your target market, competitors, costs, and the importance of delivering value to your clients.

One of the key takeaways of this chapter is that photographers need to learn how to communicate their pricing effectively to their clients. It's not just about the number you put on your services, it's also about the manner in which you present it. By following the advice in this chapter, you can build a solid Brand Art identity and a pricing strategy that works for your business, positioning yourself for success in the highly competitive photography industry.

FART/13:

Underestimating the Importance of Pricing and Business Model

Building a successful photography business requires two key elements: your pricing and business model. However, underestimating the worth of their work and services is one of the biggest Brand Farts that photographers make.

Many photographers offer low prices for their professional work, perhaps out of a lack of confidence or a concern that they will scare off potential customers. But this can have detrimental effects on their business. When you undercharge for your services, you're telling potential customers that your artistic talent isn't worth much. This may lower the perceived value of your brand and decrease your chances of attracting high-paying customers.

On the other hand, if you charge potential clients in excess of what they will receive in return, you run the risk of turning them off, as they may believe your rates are unwarranted. Loss of business could result, which would be bad for your reputation and brand. Striking a balance between your prices and the value you are providing is the answer.

You must have a thorough understanding of your operating expenses and the distinctive value proposition that distinguishes you from your rivals to strike this balance. While considering your expenses and profit margins, you must set prices that are justified but competitive. You may need to compare your rates to those of other local photographers as a result, so do your research first.

Understanding your target market is another essential element of a successful business model for photographers. Your ideal clients are who? What do they value? What are their pain points, and how can you solve them through your photographic expertise? You can adjust your services and fees to meet the unique needs and preferences of your target audience by providing answers to these questions.

Additionally crucial is having a sound pricing strategy. This involves figuring out how much your services will cost, deciding whether to include packages and deciding how best to communicate your prices to potential clients. You must be open and honest about your rates and communicate the worth of your creative offerings.

The career of renowned photographer Ryan Brenizer represents the significance of recognising these pricing factors. Receiving numerous honours and awards for his outstanding work, Ryan's success is a result of both his sharp business acumen as well as his artistic talent.

Coming from a photojournalistic background, Ryan quickly discovered that he had a distinct style and photographic approach that he wanted to pursue further in the specific niche of wedding photography. By specialising in one sector, he was able to develop a deep understanding of his clients' needs and tailor his services accordingly. He was able to command a higher price for his services as a result, which simultaneously helped him stand out from the competition.

Ryan acknowledged the importance of pricing his services based on his value proposition. He recognised that his work involved more than just documenting beautiful moments; it also required giving his clients an unforgettable experience. He charged a premium for his expertise, enabling him to buy top-of-the-line equipment and give his newlywed customers a level of professionalism that was unmatched.

Ryan's early adoption of a scalable business model was another crucial decision. Ryan came to the realisation that if he wanted to expand his company, he could not handle everything on his own. In 2016, he merged his business with that of wedding photographer Tatiana Breslow, who would later become his wife. This resulted in the creation of their business, "The Brenizer," which provides clients with a double-threat photography experience not just on the wedding day, but with communication throughout the entire planning process and beyond.

To free up his time to concentrate on what he loves doing best, capturing stunning images, Ryan also focused on assigning tasks like post-processing, album design, and customer service to a full-time employee. This made it possible for him to serve more clients without sacrificing quality.

The success of Ryan Brenizer's photography business is a testament to the impact of understanding pricing and business model. With 1,200+ wedding bookings under their belt, Ryan together with his wife Tatiana have been able to create a flourishing photography business that is still going strong today by recognising the value of their work, concentrating on a particular market, and implementing a scalable business model.

Keep in mind, it's vital that you review and update your pricing strategy and business model frequently. Regularly evaluate your sales, costs, and profits. Base price changes on customer feedback, market trends, and demand. To learn what your clients like and don't like about your services and pricing, ask them for feedback so you can make the necessary adjustments.

FROM FART TO ART

Brand Fart

Low-priced photographers are vulnerable to damaging the perception of their brand and reducing their ability to attract individuals with high spending power. On the other hand, overcharging could cost you clients and harm your reputation. If you don't strike the right balance between pricing and value due to a lack of understanding of your target market, operating costs, and unique value proposition, it could be detrimental to your brand.

Brand Art

Building a successful photography business involves a thorough understanding of pricing and business models. To strike a balance between rates and value, you need to understand your target demographic and operating expenses, set fees that are quantifiable but competitive, and have a pricing strategy that effectively communicates the value of your services.

FART/14:

Not Differentiating Your Prices Based on Value, Quality, and Niche

To protect your profitability and brand reputation as a photographer, it's essential to correctly price your services. Failure to differentiate prices based on the value delivered, quality of craftsmanship, and market niche of each project is a typical Brand Fart photographer's commit. A one-size-fits-all strategy could result in you charging too much for simple jobs or too little for complex ones. Client dissatisfaction, decreased profitability, and a damaged image can all result from this.

You should carefully evaluate the value and quality of expertise needed for each assignment and adjust your pricing strategy as necessary to avoid making this mistake. Take into account elements like each project's complexity, duration, and target market. For instance, a premium portrait session for a musician's album cover will likely require more effort and resources than a headshot for a university student's LinkedIn profile – similar to how a personal shoot for a small business owner will likely differ from a commercial job for a major corporation in terms of requirements and expectations.

You can offer different pricing tiers that accommodate various budgets and objectives based on your judgement. For example, you can charge higher rates for premium services, and competitive prices for more basic ones. To give your clients more value and convenience, you can also create packages that combine both services and any products.

Take, for instance, the success story of Ryan and Tatiana Brenizer, who have cemented themselves as highly reputable wedding photographers by offering exceptional services and products. The couple's effective pricing strategy can be attributed to their understanding that establishing rates entails more than just covering costs and generating revenue, it involves differentiating yourself based on the value, quality, and niche of services provided.

Ryan and his wife Tatiana have created a pricing structure that accounts for the importance that their customers attach to their photography. They have designed straightforward wedding day packages with varying degrees of service that range in price from $3,750 to $6,800, which reflects their market demand. They also cater to destination wedding couples, which enables them to provide an additional tailored package that is difficult for rivals to match.

The Brenizers are aware that customers will pay more for services of exceptional quality with a unique value proposition. By placing emphasis on the calibre of their expertise, the Brenizers have created a successful business that is sought after by many clients. Their approach to pricing is an important lesson for photographers determined to differentiate themselves in a crowded market sector.

Keep in mind, whilst formulating any packages, it's critical to be open and honest about your billing policies in addition to differentiating prices based on value, quality, and niche. Your customers should be aware of the services they will receive, as well as any associated costs and fees. It's important to specify your payment conditions, including any required deposits and deadlines. It's also wise to be flexible with your rates and open to negotiation as long as the terms align with your business goals and principles.

By being transparent, you can establish trust and credibility with your clients, and prevent any misunderstandings or disputes. Additionally, you can project a professional image by showcasing your dedication to providing high-quality services and results.

SUMMARY:
FROM FART TO ART

Brand Fart

Photographers who adopt a universal pricing strategy and make the mistake of not differentiating their prices based on value and quality risk reputational damage. Failure to take into account the complexity, time frame, and target market of each project as well as the lack of a range of pricing tiers to accommodate various budgets and desired results can lead to loss of revenue and discontent for both yourself and your clients.

Brand Art

Pricing photography services accurately is a fundamental factor for photographers, as it allows them to reflect the value delivered, quality of expertise, and specialised nature of each assignment. It is crucial to evaluate criteria such as the level of work, duration, and target audience of the project to determine the most appropriate rates. By offering a range of pricing tiers, you can accommodate various budgets and desired outcomes, ensuring that clients have options that suit their needs. This approach allows photographers to strike a balance between affordability and the level of service provided, ultimately creating a win-win situation for both parties.

FART/15:

Charging for Time Not for Value

Many photographers make the mistake of believing that the time spent on a photoshoot determines its price. However, only billing for time ignores the particular impact that a photographer brings to the table. You must recognise the personal worth you provide to your clients, and charge appropriately to avoid making this Brand Fart.

Why Value-Based Pricing Is Important

Each photographer has a unique aesthetic, set of abilities, and degree of experience, all of which should be reflected in their fee. You can better express your intrinsic worth to potential customers by charging for value rather than time. Billing for merit also guarantees that the photographer's special talents and skills are appropriately respected, leading to greater satisfaction for both the creative and the client.

Here, we'll discuss how to steer clear of charging for time.

To determine the appropriate pricing for your services, it's important to consider several factors. First and foremost, critically evaluate the calibre of your work and the expertise you bring to each project. Take into account your years of experience, specialised skills, and artistic vision that gives you a competitive edge. An honest assessment will help you establish a baseline for the value you offer.

Additionally, take the time to learn about your client's needs and expectations. Every project is unique, and clients may have specific requirements or desired outcomes. By customising your services to meet their individual specifications, you show your commitment to delivering exceptional results. This tailored approach adds value to your services and justifies the pricing structure you set.

When communicating your pricing to clients, it's vital to articulate the value they can expect in return. Explain your services in detail and draw attention to the advantages and benefits they will receive. Present your portfolio of previous work to highlight your expertise and showcase the quality of your results. Including client testimonials and endorsements can further enhance your credibility and reinforce the value you bring to the table.

Percentage-Based Value Pricing

Considering the monetary value that a client will receive from your photographs and modifying your pricing accordingly is a crucial aspect of charging for value as a photographer. By aligning your fees with the client's potential profit, you can ensure that both sides benefit from the collaboration. This strategy takes into account the direct financial contribution your photos will have on the client's professional or personal success.

When evaluating the potential profit that an individual or organisation can generate from your photographic skills, it is essential to have open and honest communication. Discussing their objectives, targets, and intended use of the photographs will provide substantial insight into how much merit they place on your work. Understanding their expectations, and the possible impact your photographs will have on their profitability, will enable you to better determine a fair and reasonable pricing structure.

This can be achieved by presenting a percentage-based pricing framework, which allows you to assess the client's projected profit and calculate a percentage that reflects the amount your photographs contribute to their financial goals. The percentage can vary depending on factors such as the complexity of the project, the level of expertise required, and the exclusivity of the usage rights. Ranging from 10% to 50% of the potential profit, this model ensures that you are appropriately compensated for the value you generate.

By taking into account the customer's conceivable financial gain and adapting your pricing in accordance, you effectively showcase the intrinsic worth and influence of your photographic skills. Nevertheless, it is vital to emphasise the importance of maintaining open dialogue and transparency throughout the negotiation process. This strategy builds trust and ensures that both parties perceive the pricing structure as equitable and balanced. As a result, you position yourself as a strategic partner committed to their success, while also recognising the significance of your expertise and the potential return on investment that your work can offer.

Incorporating Equipment Rental into Value-Based Pricing

Including the hire cost of equipment within the value pricing is an important consideration for photographers who want to charge for their services based on the benefits they provide. In order to capture high-quality images and deliver the desired results for clients, photography equipment is a key factor. By incorporating the hire cost of equipment into the overall pricing structure, photographers can ensure that their clients understand and appreciate the service they receive.

Professional-grade photography equipment can be very expensive to purchase and maintain. Cameras, lenses, lighting equipment, and other accessories require significant investments. Including the rental cost of equipment in service pricing allows photographers to recover these expenses and ensure they have the funds and access to the latest and most advanced tools for their work. It also enables you to continuously upgrade your equipment and stay at the forefront of industry standards and technological advancements.

We are all conscious that the quality of equipment directly impacts the outcome of the photographs. Higher-end cameras and lenses produce sharper images with better colour accuracy and detail. Clients who value exceptional results and are willing to invest in professional photography services understand the significance of using the finest equipment. By including the hire cost of equipment in your pricing, you communicate your commitment to delivering superior results and reassure clients that they are investing in a comprehensive package that includes both skillful expertise and top-of-the-line tools.

FROM FART TO ART

Brand Fart

Ignoring value-based pricing can be a costly mistake for photographers. Relying solely on time-based pricing overlooks the unique qualities and expertise you bring to the table. By failing to incorporate the hire cost of equipment into your pricing, you risk undervaluing the quality and impact of your work. Without aligning your fees with the influence and financial potential your photography offers, you miss the opportunity to position yourself as a trusted partner invested in your client's success.

Brand Art

By transitioning from time-based pricing to value-based pricing, photographers can accurately represent their distinctive aesthetics, skills, and experience through their fees. Including the cost of equipment rental in your pricing structure illustrates your dedication to achieving outstanding results. Furthermore, aligning your pricing with the intrinsic worth and financial influence of your photographic expertise places you as a strategic partner who is fully dedicated to your client's business growth and prosperity.

FART/16:

Saying "Yes" More Than You Say "No"

It's easy to fall into the trap of accepting every job that comes your way as a professional photographer. This may appear to be a good way to expand your portfolio and earn a consistent income, but it can easily cause burnout and a loss of focus on the kinds of photography that are most important to you. Accepting low-paying jobs that don't fit your field of expertise or personal vision can also undermine your brand integrity and dilute your reputation as a professional photographer.

Sustainably growing your photography business requires careful thought and well-informed choices that are in line with your pricing model. You can avoid the Brand Fart of saying "yes" to any job and build a strong

Brand Art that draws in the right clients by putting the following steps into practice.

Aligning Clients with Your Vision and Values:
Take the time to understand your photographic aesthetic and brand identity. Define the types of clients that align with your vision and values. This will enable you to focus your efforts on serving a demographic that appreciates your unique style and expertise. By targeting the right clientele, you can avoid accepting assignments that undermine your level of ability or undervalue your services. You can position yourself as a specialist and command higher prices while providing exceptional value by catering to your ideal customers.

Clearly Define Your Availability and Rates:
Transparency is key when it comes to managing client expectations. Your pricing policy and availability should be made known in advance. This will help prospective consumers understand what to expect, and you'll be able to filter out those who cannot meet your requirements. Outline the types of projects you are open to accepting, specify your working hours, and establish the minimum fee you are willing to accept for your services. By setting these boundaries, you ensure that you only attract clients who are willing to invest in your expertise and align with your value proposition.

Think Strategically About the Jobs You Accept:

You have the power to choose the projects you take on. Instead of accepting every job that comes your way, approach your decision-making strategically. Evaluate how well each opportunity fits with your brand, area of expertise, and long-term career goals. For example, if you specialise in match-day football photography, it may be more beneficial to decline footballer portrait photography projects that fall outside your realm of expertise. By focusing on becoming the go-to live-action football photographer in your region, you can cultivate a reputation for excellence and attract clients who value your specific skills and are willing to pay your desired rates. This strategic approach allows you to maximise your time, energy, and resources on the jobs that align with your career goals and deliver the most significant impact.

By implementing these strategies, you can avoid the trap of saying "yes" to every job and instead build a thriving photography business that capitalises on your strengths, draws the right clients, and allows you to charge premium prices for the value you provide. Remember, saying "no" to certain jobs creates room for the ones that truly matter, enabling you to provide exceptional value and establish a solid reputation in your chosen photographic domain.

FROM FART TO ART

Brand Fart

Photographers who accept every project are setting themselves up for failure. Accepting any job regardless of expertise, value, or personal style puts you at risk of undervaluing your services, overworking yourself, and experiencing financial hardship. Setting unclear boundaries can also result in difficult clients who might exploit your eagerness to accept any low-paying assignment.

Brand Art

Photographers must avoid the trap of saying "yes" to every job that comes their way. By aligning customers with your vision and values, clearly defining your availability and rates, and thinking strategically about the jobs you accept, you can build a strong brand that allows you to focus on your chosen area of expertise and attracts the right clients who are happy to pay your photographic package fees.

FART/17:

Not Building Strong Relationships with Clients and Partners to Encourage Repeat Business

To encourage repeat business, photographers must cultivate strong relationships with their clients and collaborators in addition to taking stunning photos. Unfortunately, a lot of photographers commit Brand Fart by ignoring these connections, which results in lost opportunities and potential revenue.

Why It's Important to Develop Strong Relationships

For the long-term financial success of your photography Brand Art, developing trusting relationships with your customers and business partners is essential. Here are some reasons why.

Repeat Business:
When you invest in developing strong relationships with your clients and associates, they are more likely to return to you for their future photography needs. By consistently delivering exceptional service while cultivating trust, you create loyal customers and partners who value your work and who desire to work with you again. This translates to more repeat business, which creates a reliable source of revenue and a devoted clientele.

Referral Network:
Referrals play a significant role in the growth of your photography business, as satisfied clients and collaborators are more likely to recommend your services to others. By prioritising relationship-building and consistently delivering outstanding experiences, you can establish a strong rapport and create a reliable stream of new customers. Going above and beyond, meeting deadlines, and showing professionalism in all interactions, builds confidence and respect with clients. This reputation for

reliability and competence fosters trust, leading to referrals and repeat business, ultimately accelerating the expansion of your photography venture.

Opening Doors:

Good relations with business partners facilitate opportunities for collaboration. When you have solid relationships with other professionals in the industry, you can combine your talents and resources to create outstanding work that exceeds what you could achieve alone. Additionally, collaborating with trusted partners often leads to greater exposure, as they may promote and showcase this collaborative work, opening doors to new audiences and greater prospects for your photography career.

Creative Trust:

Trust serves a vital purpose in collaborations with business partners such as models, stylists, and other photographers. When you cultivate an environment of openness and confidence in one another, it encourages creative synergy and the exchange of ideas. Trust allows you to work seamlessly with others, leveraging each person's unique skills and perspectives to produce photographs that are authentic and meaningful.

The impressive track record of Ryan and Tatiana Brenizer's photography business serves as a reminder of how crucial it is to give customers a satisfying experience from the first consultation to the delivery of the final product. The Brenizers' ability to develop solid relationships with clients and business partners is a key factor in their success as wedding photographers.

Ryan and Tatiana garner word-of-mouth referrals by providing a customised experience for each of their clients. They spend the necessary time getting to know their customers to comprehend their particular wedding needs and preferences. By doing this, they are able to design a tailored service that goes above and beyond their client's expectations.

In addition to forging strong relationships with their clients, Ryan and Tatiana value their partnerships with wedding planners and other industry professionals. They are aware that these collaborations can result in new business opportunities and create long-term relationships.

Prioritising effective and clear communication with their partners before, during, and after client wedding ceremonies, Ryan and Tatiana are committed to upholding these relationships. They go the extra mile to produce outstanding work that highlights the expertise of their photography as well as the services of their partners. By doing this, they not only encourage repeat business but also broaden their network of contacts within the wedding industry.

The strategy used by Ryan and Tatiana to develop trusting relationships with clients and business partners has produced a flourishing photography business that continues to expand. Their commitment to creating a unique and exceptional experience for their clients has led to numerous referrals, whilst their partnerships with industry professionals have opened up new opportunities and facilitated business retention.

How to Develop Strong Relationships

Now that you are aware of the significance of developing great relationships, let's look at some techniques you can employ to do so.

Communication:

Building strong relationships requires effective dialogue. Make sure you communicate clearly and effectively and that you are responsive to your clients and partners. This entails being prompt in your email and phone responses and explaining project expectations in clear terms.

Personalisation:

Learn as much as you can about each client and business partner on a personal level. Keep in mind important information about their lives and hobbies and use this knowledge to tailor your communication with them. They may feel more connected to you and respected as a result of this.

Consistency:

Be consistent in your communications with clients and business partners. This calls for dependability, punctuality, and the delivery of consistently excellent service. Your clients and business partners are more likely to trust you and value your work if they know what to expect from you.

Networking:

Attend events and make connections with other professionals in your sector through networking. Solid connections with other photographers, event coordinators, and studios can open up new possibilities and opportunities for collaboration.

Follow-Up:

As soon as a project is finished, make sure to get in touch with your clients and business partners to express your gratitude and find out if they have any additional photography needs. This could lead to repeat business and the preservation of the relationship.

For your photography brand pricing strategy to be successful, you need to have solid relationships with your clients and business partners. By nurturing these connections, you cultivate trust, loyalty, and satisfaction, which in turn allows you to confidently set prices that reflect the value you bring to your clients. Building strong relationships produces a solid foundation for repeat business, referrals, and collaborations, enhancing your reputation and positioning you as a trusted and sought-after photographer. Investing in these relationships not only contributes to your financial success, but also elevates your creative brand and establishes your name in a competitive market.

FROM FART TO ART

Brand Fart

Neglecting to build strong relationships with clients and partners can have a negative impact on your photography business's pricing plan. Disregarding these connections results in lost opportunities for referrals, collaborations, and ultimately repeat business, which helps you establish your rates with confidence. By failing to invest in relationship-building, you miss out on the potential revenue, growth, and reputation enhancement that come with loyal customers and satisfied collaborators.

Brand Art

Strong connections with clients and creative partners are essential for any photography business's pricing model. Establishing loyal clientele and collaborators through effective communication, personalisation, consistency, networking, and following-up, results in repeat business, referrals, creative trust, and ultimately more financial opportunities. Building relationships is just as important as capturing amazing images.

FART/18:

Neglecting to Re-evaluate and Adapt Your Pricing and Business Model

To be successful as a professional photographer, you must have a firm grasp of your pricing and business model. However, simply setting a pricing strategy and forgetting about it can be detrimental to your brand.

Let's explore why continuously re-evaluating and adapting your pricing and business model is crucial for your success, and how to avoid this common Brand Fart.

Failure to evaluate and modify your rates and operational model could have damaging consequences. The photography industry is constantly evolving, so what worked in the past might not be relevant today. For instance, the perceived value of professional photography has decreased as a result of the rise in popularity of digital and smartphone photography, which has made it easier for people to take their own pictures. Failure to adjust to these changes could lead to lost sales, a decline in clientele, and ultimately a failing business.

Continuously re-evaluating and adapting your photography fees and business model not only helps you stay competitive but also presents opportunities for growth, innovation, and attracting new clients. For example, if you have been offering moody headshot services to actors for several years but observe a shift in client preference towards clean backdrop portrait photography for their LinkedIn profiles, it may be wise to consider launching new packages and updating your pricing structure to meet this evolving demand.

By paying close attention to market trends and customer desires, you can identify emerging opportunities and make informed decisions to transform your business approach and rates accordingly. This proactive attitude allows you to meet the evolving needs of your niche market, stay ahead of the competition, and position your photography company for long-term success.

Methods to Remain Competitive

What are the key strategies to ensure your pricing and business model align with industry changes?

Data-Driven Decision-Making:
Routinely reviewing your financial data, such as revenue and expenses, enables you to identify trends and changes within your company. This valuable information serves as a compass for making calculated decisions regarding your pricing strategy and operational framework. By analysing the patterns and shifts in your finances, you gain insights into the effectiveness of your current approach and can determine if adjustments are necessary. This diligent monitoring empowers you to confidently navigate the dynamic business environment, ensuring that your pricing remains competitive and your operating system remains aligned with your overall objectives.

Customer-Driven Transformation:
In order to revise and adapt your pricing and business model, gathering customer feedback is essential. You can learn a lot about your customers' preferences and opinions by using a variety of techniques, such as conducting surveys, setting up focus groups, or simply getting in touch with them directly. This knowledge enables you to take well-informed actions and modify your photography rates and business structure to better meet their needs.

Understanding what customers appreciate and what aspects of your services they may dislike allows you to refine and improve your offerings, fostering stronger customer satisfaction and loyalty. By actively listening to your audience, you can stay responsive to their changing expectations and make sure that your photography fees and business strategy continue to be customer-centric and competitive in the market.

Innovation-Driven Adaptation:

By actively participating in photography conferences, regularly reading industry publications, and staying on top of the latest innovations, you can position yourself as an informed and forward-thinking professional photographer. These proactive efforts allow you to stay on top of market trends, industry developments, and emerging techniques. This valuable knowledge equips you with the insights needed to make strategic decisions and structure your business in a way that aligns with current market demands. Whether it's identifying emerging opportunities, embracing technological advancements, or anticipating shifts in consumer behaviour, staying educated about market movements empowers you to make wise choices and navigate the evolving landscape of the photography industry with confidence.

While changing your pricing and business model can present challenges, doing so is essential to the survival and growth of your photography company. You can avoid the common Brand Fart of failing to re-evaluate your pricing structure and business approach by routinely reviewing your financials, getting customer feedback, and keeping up with market trends. Your photography business will succeed and expand if you adopt the appropriate strategy to stay competitive and satisfy the evolving needs of your target market.

SUMMARY:
FROM FART TO ART

Brand Fart

Failure to evaluate and modify your pricing and business model can lead to missed opportunities and slow growth. If you don't adapt your strategy to fit shifting customer needs and market trends, as a photographer, you will eventually fall behind your competition and suffer financially.

Brand Art

The success of your photography business depends on developing a pricing strategy and business plan that are consistent with your brand identity and values. You can stay competitive while upholding the reputation of your company and your premium services by making well-informed decisions based on market trends and the needs of your target audience.

BRAND FART MARKETING

┌ ┐
└ ┘

In today's fast-paced world, social media has developed into a vital tool for photography brands to showcase their creativity and connect with their target audience. Social media platforms such as Instagram and X Social provide photographers with an opportunity to exhibit their work and cultivate brand awareness among a vast online audience.

However, there is a significant difference between using social media for Brand Fart and using it for Brand Art. Social media can help photography businesses build a distinctive brand identity and draw in potential clients, but if used improperly, it can also damage their reputation.

Like many other photographers, Instagram was my preferred platform for showcasing my work. As my career progressed and my network and following expanded, I recognised the importance of staying active on social media to maintain brand awareness and attract new clients. Being an introvert and a private person by nature, it was initially difficult for me to put myself out there, since it's far easier to be behind the camera than in front of it.

Despite that, I utilised social media tools and leveraged video marketing to amplify my brand message and share behind-the-scenes footage of my studio and travelling shoot work, as well as my photographer and influencer partnerships. Gradually, Instagram became my primary channel for bookings, collaborations, and client communication.

My process, however, was completely derailed in January 2021 when my photography Instagram account was disabled without warning. Despite my efforts to recover it, after two months I realised that I had no choice but to start from scratch with a new account. This experience taught me the importance of having a portfolio website, where I could take control of my digital brand presence.

As I began to implement my new online strategy, I was surprised to discover that many photographers do not have a website, and those who do often overlook the importance of optimising it for search engines. With a solid website in place, photographers can use social media to complement and promote their brands, resulting in a more cohesive and fruitful web marketing strategy.

In this chapter, we will delve into the dos and don'ts of digital marketing for photographers. How to create an active online community and steer clear of common social media marketing Brand Farts will also be covered. By mastering the art of social media outreach and utilising a mobile-friendly website, photographers can create a strong Brand Art identity and elevate their web presence, allowing them to connect with a broader audience and attract desired clients.

FART/19:

Not Building a Strong Online Presence

As a photographer, you may have incredible talent and produce beautiful images, but without a strong online presence in your niche, potential clients may not even know you exist. In today's digital age, having a professional and well-designed website, an active social media presence, and a portfolio that features your finest work is crucial for establishing your Brand Art.

Why Photographers Need to Build a Strong Online Presence

Establishes Your Brand:

When people search for you online, your website and social media profiles are frequently the first things they see. Having a polished, well-designed online presence can help you build your Brand Art and convey your values, aesthetics and photographic philosophy.

Displays Your Work:

Through your online portfolio, you have the opportunity to share your creative talent with the world. By showcasing your best work, and displaying your versatility within your niche, including a variety of styles and artistic expressions, you not only highlight your technical proficiency but also illustrate your creative vision and ability to capture a range of subjects. This allows potential clients to get a comprehensive view of your capabilities and increases their confidence when hiring you.

Helps You Reach New Clients:

A strong online presence can help you reach new customers who might not have found you otherwise. With an up-to-date website and being active on social media, you can connect with potential clients and build a community of followers who appreciate your work and spread the word about it.

Shows Off Your Expertise:

You can exhibit your knowledge and win over prospective clients by having a well-constructed online profile. By consistently producing valuable content and interacting with your audience on social media platforms, you can effectively showcase your expertise and establish yourself as a trusted resource in the photography community.

Fashion photographer Jessica Kobeissi is a prime example of a creative who has built a strong online presence in her niche. She has been able to establish herself as an authority in her field and amass a devoted fan base by imparting all of her expertise to her 1.9 million+ subscribers through her YouTube channel, which is dedicated to sharing educational tips, tutorials, and behind-the-scenes footage from her photoshoots. More importantly, potential clients looking for a photographer with her skills and experience have been drawn to her by the exceptional educational material she has published.

In addition to YouTube, Jessica has a solid representation on social media platforms like Instagram and X Social. She exhibits her photography work on Instagram and gives her 500K+ audience a peek into her creative process which highlights her abilities. She has been able to build a large following on the platform through her consistent delivery of high-quality content that is in line with her brand. She also interacts with her followers on X Social, shares her thoughts and opinions on matters relating to photography, and advertises her work and upcoming projects.

Jessica has developed an impressive digital footprint thanks in large part to her consistent and genuine Brand Art. All of her online platforms maintain a uniform and clear brand identity, which accurately represents her personality and values, and enables her to engage her target demographic more deeply. She has established a solid name for herself in her market and attracted clients who appreciate her distinct aesthetic and method of approaching photography by remaining true to her brand, whilst repeatedly producing work of exceptional quality.

How to Establish a Strong Online Presence

Present Your Portfolio:

Your website should serve as the focal point of your online presence and operate as the centrepiece of your portfolio, which should contain high-quality images of your finest work. To make it easier for potential clients to find what they're looking for, implement an intuitive layout and arrange your photographs by style, genre, or location.

Consistency is the Key:

Social media is a fantastic tool for connecting with potential clients, sharing your work, and growing a following. Be consistent in your posting and engagement on the platforms that are most appropriate for your niche and audience.

Communicate Your Knowledge:

By sharing tutorials, tips, and valuable insights through various channels such as blog articles, long and short-form videos, and social media posts, you can showcase your industry knowledge and position yourself as a credible authority in your field.

Monitor Your Progress:

The performance of your online presence must be measured and tracked to determine what is effective and what is not. Google Analytics is a fantastic tool that can assist you in measuring the traffic, page views, bounce rates, and other crucial data for your website. You can determine which pages are performing well, which ones need improvement, and which marketing tactics are generating the most traffic by analysing these metrics. You can monitor your followers, engagement levels, and other important information using social media analytics. This can assist you in determining which social media sites are most effective for your business and help you adjust your strategy as necessary.

SUMMARY:
FROM FART TO ART

Brand Fart

Neglecting to establish a robust online presence and solely prioritising the creation of stunning images can have detrimental branding implications. Without a strong digital footprint, prospective clients may remain unaware of your existence, and the failure to actively share your expertise and monitor statistical analytics can result in missed opportunities for growth and engagement.

Brand Art

For you to effectively market your photography brand, reach a larger audience, and establish yourself as a knowledgeable and reputable professional in the field, you must develop a solid online presence across a variety of web platforms. It is essential to strike a balance between producing compelling visuals and actively cultivating your digital standing to maximise your brand's visibility and attract promising possibilities for employment.

FART/20:

Choosing Not to Be Active on Social Media

Having a strong online presence is essential for photographers in today's digital world to develop their Brand Art and expand their businesses. Instagram, Facebook, and X Social are just a few examples of social media sites that can be extremely effective marketing tools for reaching your target market, showcasing your work, and cultivating connections with potential clients.

Here are some reasons why being inactive on social media is a big Brand Fart for photographers, and some insights on how to use social media effectively.

Visibility:

Visibility is a critical aspect of social media presence for photographers. In a saturated market with numerous photographers vying for clients' attention, it becomes challenging for prospective customers to find you if you are idle on social channels. To overcome this hurdle, it is essential to remain active and engaged on the social networking sites where your target demographic hangs out. By consistently sharing your work, interacting with your market, and participating in relevant communities, you increase your exposure and improve the likelihood of being discovered by potential clients. It is important to understand your audience's social preferences and habits to effectively pinpoint the platforms they use frequently, ensuring that you remain visible and accessible to those who are seeking photography services.

Establishing Trust and Credibility:

Earning trust and building credibility is vital for photographers, and social media platforms offer an ideal avenue to achieve this. Consistently delivering high-quality content and engaging with your audience's comments and enquiries can instill a sense of trust and authenticity, positioning you as a reliable and reputable photographer. As you develop legitimacy through your digital footprint, prospective customers are more likely to view you as a respected professional, increasing the likelihood that they will choose to hire you for their photography needs. Social media serves as a powerful tool to establish and reinforce your reputation, ultimately influencing potential clients' decisions in favour of working with you.

Cost-Effective Marketing:

Social media provides a budget-friendly and powerful marketing avenue for photographers to promote their business and reach a large audience. Producing and sharing high-quality content on social media networks allows you to effectively promote your services without incurring substantial expenses associated with traditional advertising methods. Photographers can boost their brand's visibility, bring in more business, and cultivate relationships with their audience by strategically using social media tools like hashtags and targeted campaigns. This cost-effective marketing approach provides you with a valuable opportunity to grow your business whilst building a strong online presence in the competitive photography industry.

Staying Ahead of The Competition:

Expanding your knowledge and staying ahead of the competition is vital for photographers, and social media provides an invaluable vehicle for achieving these goals. By actively following and communicating with other photographers and industry experts on social media platforms, you gain access to a wealth of information and wisdom, whilst staying updated on the latest techniques, trends, and best practices in the photography industry. This exposure to diverse perspectives and expertise allows you to continually improve your skills, broaden your creative horizons, and enhance the quality of your work. Utilising social media as a tool for ongoing education and professional development positions you as a knowledgeable and innovative photographer, drawing clients who value your dedication to staying ahead of the curve.

SUMMARY:
FROM FART TO ART

Brand Fart

Photographers who disregard the value of having a consistent social media presence give up on the opportunity to develop their brand and scale their business. You lose out on the chance to connect with your target audience, build rapport and credibility with prospective clients, present your work and photographic vision, and remain one step ahead of the competition by not being active on the social channels where your market resides.

Brand Art

In today's digital landscape, photographers must prioritise their social media activity as a fundamental aspect of their marketing strategy to effectively expand their business and thrive in the online realm. By producing engaging content, and consistently interacting with your audience, you can leverage the power of social media to enhance your visibility, attract new clients, and keep ahead of market developments.

FART/21:

Underutilising Video Marketing

You have an impressive portfolio of images that illustrate your abilities as a photographer. However, in today's crowded marketplace, simply having an online gallery of beautiful photographs may not be enough to stand out from the competition. For this reason, you should utilise video marketing to strengthen your Brand Art and attract new clients.

Why is Video Marketing Important for Photographers?

Showcases Your Personality and Style:
You can show off your personality and sense of style as a photographer through visual marketing. Video media is an effective tool for helping your audience get to know you and your brand, whether you use it to share your photographic process, create behind-the-scenes vlogs, or exhibit your work.

Increases Engagement and Attracts a Following:
Video footage is highly shareable, and viewers are more likely to engage with and circulate videos than other types of media. As a result, using visual content to grow a following and interact with your target market is highly recommended.

Reaches a Wider Audience:
You can reach more people with visual media than with conventional marketing strategies. You can easily connect with a global audience thanks to platforms like TikTok, Instagram Reels, and YouTube Shorts, which will help you develop your Brand Art.

Highlights Your Work in a Unique Way:
Through video advertising, you can present your work uniquely and memorably. Create a short film that showcases your camera skills and editing talent, or make

a dynamic slideshow using your photographs. You can use video to bring your work to life in a way that is just not possible with still images.

Helps Make a Name for Yourself:

You can establish yourself as an authority in your niche by producing and distributing high-quality visual content. Video is a great way to highlight your abilities and position yourself as a leader in your industry, whether you choose to teach others about your knowledge and expertise through tutorials or by displaying your work.

Jessica Kobeissi is an example of a photographer who has effectively used video marketing to build her personal brand. She publishes valuable content on her YouTube channel, such as her photography journey and Q&A sessions. Jessica has developed an engaged and passionate following as a result of her consistent creation of informative and educational content, which has enhanced her Brand Art and attracted high-calibre clients.

Likewise, Jessica employs video marketing on Instagram, among other social media sites. On Instagram, she shares Reels of her photoshoots and behind-the-scenes footage, providing her followers with a glimpse into her creative process and photographic philosophy whilst spotlighting her talents.

Utilising visual media to highlight her experience and photography knowledge, Jessica has also collaborated with companies to develop sponsored content to advance their brands. She's broadened her viewership by working with organisations like Adobe and Squarespace, and she has earned a reputation as a respected expert in her field.

By openly sharing her thoughts, opinions, and private experiences on camera, Jessica has nurtured authenticity and trust with her followers and developed a strong relationship with her audience through video marketing. As a result, she has amassed a devoted core base that not only appreciates her work but also spreads the word about it, further establishing her Brand Art.

How Can Photographers Start Taking Advantage of Video Marketing?

Target Your Demographic:
To effectively leverage video marketing as a photographer, it's crucial to consider the online characteristics, interests, and preferences of your target demographic. For instance, if you specialise in live music event photography, your ideal client might include music festivals, concert venues, or even individual musicians or bands. You could create highlight reels of your live music photography, showcasing the energy and excitement of performances. You can also capture interviews with

musicians, behind-the-scenes footage of sound-checks and rehearsals, and visually engaging montages that capture the essence of the music event experience. By tailoring your video content to the interests and tastes of your target audience, you can attract their attention and establish yourself as the go-to photographer for your area of expertise.

Create a Content Plan:

Once you have identified your demographic, it's time to develop a content plan for your videos. Think about the message you want to convey and the goals you want to achieve through your visual footage. Consider the types of media that align with your brand personality and photography aesthetic. Using the live music event photographer for example, you could create a content plan for a series of videos that provide tips and insights on capturing the best live music shots, or artist profiles that showcase the unique style and performances of different musicians or bands. It's important to ensure that your content is relevant, engaging, and authentic, reflecting your unique personality and skills as a photographer.

Get Your Videos Noticed:

After producing your videos, it's crucial to promote and distribute them effectively to get noticed by your target audience. Start by featuring your visuals prominently on your website, creating a dedicated video gallery or embedding them within relevant blog articles.

Leverage the power of social media platforms to share your videos with your followers. Post them on platforms like YouTube, TikTok, or Instagram, and use engaging captions and tags to enhance discoverability. Encourage your followers to repost and share your videos with their networks, amplifying the reach and exposure of your content.

SUMMARY:

FROM FART TO ART

Brand Fart

Many photographers frequently overlook video marketing, as they believe that their portfolio is enough to differentiate them from the competition. By failing to use visual footage to exhibit your work and broaden your market reach, you are in danger of becoming just another face in the crowd and losing out on valuable opportunities to expand your audience and strengthen your brand image.

Brand Art

In a fiercely competitive market, effective video advertising can significantly assist photographers in creating a unique brand that sets them apart from competitors. You can show off your personality, connect with a larger audience, highlight your work distinctively, and establish yourself as an expert in your field by implementing visual marketing strategies.

FART/22:

Not Having a Mobile-Friendly Website: Instagram Is Not Your Portfolio

A website that displays your work and makes it simple for potential clients to contact you is fundamental if you intend to be a successful Brand Art photographer. However, a lot of photographers make the Brand Fart error of not having a website or having a website that's not mobile-friendly, which can hurt their reputation and employment prospects.

In the modern digital era, having a website is a must for photographers looking to showcase their work and attract potential clients. A website serves as an online portfolio that enables photographers to exhibit their best photographs and provide details on their services, rates, and contact information. Not having a website can make it challenging for prospective consumers to find and learn more about your profession, which could ultimately result in lost job opportunities.

Additionally, having a website that looks great and works well across all devices is essential in today's world, where more people than ever before access the internet via their smartphones. A website that's difficult to navigate or use on a mobile handset can be frustrating for potential clients and may make them less likely to book your services.

Here are some key reasons why having a mobile-friendly website is important for photographers.

Improved User Experience:
A mobile-friendly photography website that's responsive and easily navigable is essential for providing an optimal user experience. It ensures that visitors can browse through your portfolio and access relevant information seamlessly, without facing any frustrations or difficulties. By providing a smooth and enjoyable browsing encounter, you enhance the chances of capturing the attention and interest of prospective consumers, keeping them engaged with your work, and increasing the likelihood of them reaching out to enquire about your photographic services.

Greater Visibility:

Having a mobile-optimised website for your photography business can significantly improve your online presence and boost your chances of being discovered by potential clients. Search engines, such as Google, consider mobile-friendliness as a ranking factor in their algorithms. When someone searches for photographers or related services in your area of expertise, a website that is optimised for mobile devices is more likely to appear higher in result pages. This increased visibility can have a significant impact on your exposure and brand awareness. It allows you to reach a broader audience and capitalise on the growing number of people who primarily use mobile devices for online searches.

Greater Control:

It's a mistake that could harm your brand and your chances of landing jobs, relying solely on Instagram or other social media platforms as your online portfolio. With a mobile-friendly website, you have complete control over how your work is displayed and how people can interact with you. It enables you to display your portfolio in a way that highlights your style and your brand message, and you can easily add information about your photographic packages and pricing, as well as having a contact form that makes it simple for potential clients to get in touch with you.

Better Branding:

Having a mobile-friendly website allows you to establish and reinforce your Brand Art in the digital space. Your website serves as a visual representation of your creative business and acts as an online vehicle for presenting your unique style, artistic vision, and brand voice. By designing your website with your brand in mind, you can create a cohesive and consistent internet footprint that aligns with your photography identity. Customising the layout, colour scheme, typography, and overall aesthetics of your website to match your brand's personality helps you to stand out from the competition. A well-crafted mobile-friendly website that reflects your brand narrative becomes an extension of your photography portfolio, leaving a lasting impression on visitors. This attention to detail not only enhances your professional image but also attracts clients who resonate with your photographic approach and values.

FROM FART TO ART

Brand Fart

Photographers who fail to have a website that is compatible with mobile devices are seriously damaging their brand. A bad website design that misrepresents your photography business can lead to lost opportunities and a decline in bookings. Solely focusing on social media platforms like Instagram to showcase and market your portfolio reduces your control over how your work is presented and how people can engage with your brand.

Brand Art

Photographers who want to build a solid digital marketing footprint that accurately represents their brand and highlights their work must have a mobile-friendly website. Regardless of the device they're using, a mobile-responsive site makes it simple for potential clients to access your portfolio, contact information, and other important information.

FART/23:

Underestimating the Importance of Search Engine Optimisation (SEO)

For your photography Brand Art, it is essential that you understand the significance of Search Engine Optimisation (SEO). Your website and online content must be optimised for SEO to appear higher on Search Engine Results Pages (SERPs) for relevant keywords. The higher you rank, the more likely it is that people looking for a photographer in your niche will find your website.

Let's explore the reasons why SEO is important for your photography business and go through some key strategies to help you optimise your website for search engines.

Why SEO is Important for Building Your Photography Brand

SEO Helps in Increasing Customer Attraction:
Whilst having a solid portfolio, a vibrant social media presence, and stellar reviews are valuable, they may not be enough to distinguish yourself from the competition without the help of Search Engine Optimisation. SEO plays a crucial role in increasing customer attraction by ensuring that your photography business stands out from the competition in online search results. By executing effective SEO practices, such as keyword research, on-page optimisation, and link building, you can improve your website's prominence and ranking in search engine results, capturing a wave of individuals who are seeking photography services in which you specialise.

SEO Builds Your Credibility and Authority:
The fact that you appear higher in organic search results for relevant keywords indicates your level of expertise in your industry in the minds of potential clients and website visitors. When your photography business consistently ranks well in SERPs, it sends a clear message that you are a trusted and reputable authority in your field. This increased exposure and credibility not only draws in more organic traffic to your website but also instills confidence in your audience, leading to higher conversion rates and inevitably more business opportunities.

SEO Increases Your Digital Footprint:

With the daily high demand for photography services on search engines, creatives must have a strong online presence if they want to capture fresh business. Implementing effective SEO strategies allows photographers to improve their online visibility and expand their reach to a broader audience. By optimising your website and content for relevant keywords, you can increase your organic search rankings and appear prominently in SERPs. As a result, photographers can attract more website traffic, generate leads, and ultimately convert them into paying customers.

The Most Effective Techniques for Search Engine Optimisation

Optimise Your Website Structure:

Create a seamless user experience by optimising your website structure. Ensure that your menu is clean and well-organised, allowing visitors to navigate through different sections effortlessly. Additionally, use concise and informative page titles that accurately represent the content they link to. Make sure to pay attention to meta descriptions, as they serve as clear summaries of each page and can greatly impact search engine visibility and click-through rates. By prioritising these aspects, you can enhance user engagement and improve the overall effectiveness of your website.

Conduct Keyword Research:

Understanding the search terms people use to find photographers in your niche will help you rank higher in search engine results. You can find the keywords that are relevant to your photography business and assess their level of competition with the help of tools like SEMrush and Google Keyword Planner. By optimising your website and content to align with high-ranking and low-competition keywords, you can enhance your online visibility and attract targeted traffic to your photography services.

Create High-Quality Content:

Both potential clients and search engines appreciate original, high-calibre material. Establishing your expertise and enhancing your online presence can be accomplished by blogging about subjects associated with your niche, producing video tutorials, and exhibiting your work. To assist search engines in understanding the subject of each page, make sure to incorporate keywords throughout your website content.

Utilise Alt Tags and Captions:

Alt tags and captions are pieces of HTML code that describe images on your website. These tags help search engines understand the content of your pictures and can help improve your website's ranking. Make sure to use relevant and descriptive alt tags and captions for each photograph on your site.

Build Quality Backlinks:

Backlinks are links pointing to your website from other websites. The more high-quality backlinks you have, the more authoritative your website appears to search engines, and the higher it will rank in search results. Ask credible websites in your area of interest to link to your site by reaching out to them, or produce excellent content that other websites will naturally want to link to.

By implementing these Search Engine Optimisation strategies, you can strengthen your online presence, enhance your website's visibility, and attract prospective customers who are actively searching for photography-related services. Keep in mind that SEO is an ongoing process, and staying updated with the latest practices and algorithm changes is essential for long-term success in the digital marketing landscape.

FROM FART TO ART

Brand Fart

Failing to prioritise SEO is a common mistake that can lead to a photographer's website dropping down the search rankings, resulting in missed opportunities. Without adequate optimisation, your brand may fall behind competitors, and potential clients who are searching for creative professionals in your niche may overlook your website.

Brand Art

Search Engine Optimisation is an essential part of a flourishing photography business. As a photographer, you can increase your online visibility and draw in new clients who are looking for your particular services by optimising your website for search engines. This can be achieved by implementing various SEO strategies and techniques such as researching and integrating keywords, producing quality content, utilising meta descriptions, applying descriptive alt tags, and building strong backlinks.

FART/24:

Neglecting Influencer Marketing and Collaborations

One of the biggest Brand Farts you can make as a photographer is to ignore influencer marketing and collaborations. Influencer marketing has become an integral part of any effective marketing strategy, and photography businesses are no exception given the billions of users who are active on social media.

Here are some pointers to help you stay clear from the Brand Fart of ignoring influencer marketing and partnerships.

Identify Influencers in Your Niche:
Investing time in thorough research and analysis is essential for determining content creators who possess

a significant and active following within your specific area of interest. It's important to seek out social media personalities whose principles, aesthetics, and target market mesh well with yours. This alignment is vital as it ensures authenticity and resonance with your intended audience. Additionally, identifying influencers who have a track record of successful collaborations with other photography brands is paramount. Their previous partnerships illustrate their ability to effectively endorse services or products, making them valuable allies in expanding your brand's reach and online impact.

Engage With Influencers:

Once you have named potential influencers, it's time to start engaging with them on social media platforms. By liking, commenting, and sharing their posts, you can show your sincere interest in their online material. Engaging with content creators in a meaningful way helps you establish a connection and increases the likelihood of getting noticed. By actively participating in conversations, offering valuable insights, and showing support, you can develop mutually beneficial relationships with influencers. Remember, rather than just promoting your brand, the objective is to forge an authentic connection. Work on developing a rapport and emphasising your genuine enthusiasm for their work.

Partner With Influencers:

Collaborating with influencers can be an effective way to establish your brand, promote your work, and expand your audience. Consider various partnership opportunities, such as joint photoshoots, workshops, or social media content collaborations. For instance, you could work with a content creator to make behind-the-scenes videos showing your photography process or organise a workshop together where you can both impart your knowledge. This can increase the visibility of your brand by utilising the individual's existing audience and leveraging their credibility and reach. Make sure the partnership fits your objectives and that the influencer's personality and principles are compatible with your brand's.

Be Ready to Invest:

It's important to recognise that influencer marketing can be an expensive strategy, particularly when working with content creators who have a sizeable fan base and clout. However, bear in mind that if you do your research well and pick the appropriate social media personalities for your brand, the return on investment could be substantial. Consider factors such as the relevance of the influencer's audience to your target market, the engagement rates on their content, and the potential reach and impact they can provide. Working with the right influencers can help you increase brand awareness, audience reach, and the possibility of gaining new customers, so be prepared to invest in influencer marketing as part of your overall marketing strategy.

Influencer marketing and collaborations provide a powerful platform for reaching and engaging with your target audience. By leveraging the reputation and online community of influencers in your niche, you can elevate your brand, increase your visibility, and ultimately grow your photography business. Embrace this impactful strategy to stay ahead in the competitive photography industry and ensure the long-term success of your Brand Art.

FROM FART TO ART

Brand Fart

Disregarding the power of influencer marketing and collaborations can be a major setback for photographers. By neglecting this strategic vehicle, you miss out on valuable opportunities to tap into the established and loyal followings of content creators, who can effectively promote your work, expand your reach, and enhance your brand visibility.

Brand Art

Influencer marketing and collaborations are powerful strategies for photographers to connect and engage with their target demographic, showcase their work, and establish a positive online image in their specialised field. You can cement yourself as a reputable professional in the industry, broaden your network, and develop your business by strategically selecting content creator partnerships that are consistent with your brand message and values.

FART/25:

Choosing Not to Network with Other Photographers

The importance of networking with other photographers in your field for developing a successful Brand Art cannot be emphasised enough. Whether you're just starting out or you're already an established professional, networking can help you create a solid reputation, make worthwhile connections, and expand your business in ways you might not have previously imagined. But many photographers are guilty of ignoring this crucial component of their career growth, which can reduce their chances of excelling, and prevent them from realising their full potential.

Networking with other photographers is essential for your Brand Art marketing efforts. Here are some reasons why you should never underestimate its importance.

Exchange of Knowledge and Ideas:

Networking with other photographers enables you to exchange knowledge and insights, pick up new skills, and find inspiration. You can gain access to a wealth of information that will enable you to advance both your professional and business endeavours by establishing connections with your peers.

Collaboration Opportunities:

Networking with other photographers can lead to collaboration opportunities. Working together on a project, photoshoot, or new business venture can bring fresh energy and life to your work. By working together, you can take advantage of each other's strengths to produce something truly unique and remarkable.

Referrals and Word-of-Mouth:

One of the most significant advantages of networking with other photographers is the potential for referrals and word-of-mouth endorsements. The likelihood that you'll be referred to clients or colleagues can be increased by developing strong relationships with other photographers in your field. This can expand your clientele and solidify your standing as a reliable and skilled photographer.

Access to New Markets and Audiences:

By networking with other photographers, you can increase your exposure and gain access to audiences and markets that you might not have otherwise been able to access. You can accomplish your goals and expand your business with the help of the contacts and resources you make through industry relationship building.

Recognising its crucial role in building a successful photography brand, professional photographers like Jessica Kobeissi have leveraged networking to their advantage. One way Jessica has accomplished this is by collaborating with other photographers in her niche, which has enabled her to cultivate relationships with like-minded creatives and enhance her brand.

She has worked closely with many credible photographers to produce "4 Photographers," a photography shoot challenge on her popular YouTube channel, exposing her to new audiences whilst showcasing the talent of her collaborators. By working with other photographers, Jessica has not only been introduced to their online communities, but has also gained new skills and techniques, enabling her to grow as an artist and enhance the quality of her work over time.

In addition to collaborations, Jessica attends photography conferences and events such as 'ProFusion

Expo' to interact face-to-face with other creatives, forming a solid network of contacts within the industry that has been significant in growing her Brand Art. Networking has helped Jessica tap into new audiences, attract attention to her work, and build strong relationships with other photographers, all of which have contributed to strengthening her brand marketing initiatives and establishing her photography brand as a reputable and influential presence in the market.

So, how can you get started with networking to enhance your brand marketing endeavours? Here are a few tips.

Attend Photography Workshops and Events:
Photography-related events are great places to meet other photographers who share your passion. Whether you're interested in attending a trade show, participating in a workshop, or joining a local photography club, these events offer an ideal opportunity to network and connect with other creatives in your specialised area.

Join Online Photography Communities:
Online forums and communities are excellent places for photographers to interact, exchange ideas, and establish connections. You can find opportunities to communicate with other photographers and share concepts by joining a photography forum, Facebook group, or subreddit.

Reach Out to Other Photographers:

Do not be hesitant to make contact with other photographers if you admire what they do. Reach out to them to ask for advice, propose a project collaboration, or simply introduce yourself. You may be surprised by the positive response you receive.

In essence, networking empowers photographers to create a web of connections that can significantly impact their brand's marketing efforts. By partnering, sharing knowledge, and building bonds within the industry, you strengthen your brand's exposure, authority, and potential for success.

Networking with fellow photographers can also help keep you inspired and motivated. Speaking with creatives who appreciate photography as much as you do has the ability to leave you energised and driven to achieve your objectives. You might even come across a mentor or someone who can provide guidance as your brand expands.

SUMMARY:
FROM FART TO ART

Brand Fart
Failure to network with other photographers in your niche is a common mistake that can prevent photographers from building successful and memorable brands. By choosing not to collaborate and share knowledge, you miss out on the chance to enhance your brand's marketing efforts, valuable opportunities to increase visibility, develop new professional relationships, and gain new insights and skills.

Brand Art
Establishing connections with other photographers who share your specialised field is a fundamental element of crafting an effective brand marketing strategy. By collaborating, exchanging insights, and engaging in online communities, you not only cultivate enduring relationships but also amplify your brand's visibility and potential business prospects.

FART/26:

Not Measuring and Analysing Your Marketing Efforts

As a photographer, you put a lot of time, energy, and money into marketing with the intention of expanding your clientele and your business. But just aimlessly throwing your brand promotion efforts into the world and hoping for the best won't cut it. To truly succeed, it's vital that you measure and analyse your marketing initiatives to understand what's working, what's not, and what needs to be changed.

Many photographers skip over this important step and just follow their instincts, making Brand Fart decisions based more on feelings and intuition than on hard facts. This may result in ineffective advertising tactics, missed opportunities, and lost income.

Why You Need to Measure and Analyse Your Marketing Efforts

For your success as a photographer, it is imperative that you measure and analyse your marketing efforts for several reasons. Let's explore some of the reasons in detail.

Unlock Your Audience Insights:
Understanding your market and what appeals to them can be accomplished through measuring and analysing your marketing initiatives. By tracking and evaluating your promotional efforts, you can unlock valuable consumer insights that are essential for your success as a photographer. Measuring key metrics such as website traffic, social media engagement, and email outreach performance allows you to obtain an in-depth understanding of your audience's preferences, behaviours, and characteristics. This important information enables you to tailor your marketing strategies and content to better resonate with your target demographic, increasing the effectiveness of your campaigns and ultimately attracting more potential clients.

Optimise Campaign Performance:
Measuring and analysing your marketing efforts allows you to optimise your outreach activities for better performance. By monitoring key metrics, you can pinpoint areas where your advertisements may be underperforming or not fulfilling your objectives. This

insight enables you to make data-driven decisions and implement improvements to enhance the effectiveness of your promotional methods. Whether it's tweaking your messaging, adjusting your targeting parameters, or refining your design content elements, examining your advertising initiatives empowers you to optimise your campaigns and achieve better outcomes.

Identify Effective Channels and Tactics:
Assessing and evaluating your marketing efforts allows you to identify effective channels and tactics, improving your Return On Investment (ROI). By tracking the performance of various marketing channels like social media, paid advertising, and email marketing, you can determine which mediums yield the highest ROI and allocate your resources accordingly. Understanding the success of specific advertising strategies, such as content material and promotional incentives, enables you to refine your approach and prioritise the methods that deliver optimal results. This helps you maximise the value of your investments and make the most of your advertising budget, ensuring that your endeavours are focused on initiatives that generate the best results.

Stay Ahead of the Competition:
Measuring and analysing your marketing efforts is essential to staying one step ahead of the competition in today's market. By monitoring industry trends, benchmarking your performance against competitors,

and identifying areas for development, you can continuously modify and refine your methods to maintain a competitive edge. Recognising what is working for your competitors and leveraging market data helps you spot opportunities and position your photography business for long-term success.

Strategies for Measuring and Analysing Your Marketing Efforts

Even though it may seem challenging, measuring and analysing your marketing endeavours can be straightforward if you use the right tools and strategies. Here are some tips to get you going.

Set Clear Goals:

Before measuring your marketing activities, it's vital to have a clear understanding of your goals. What do you want your marketing campaigns to accomplish? Whether your objective is to gain new clients, enhance brand awareness, or increase revenue, having defined targets will make it easier to track your success and quantify your progress.

Use Analytic Tools:

Utilise analytical software to monitor and assess your marketing efforts. There are many various free and paid tools available, such as Google Analytics, that allow you to monitor website traffic, measure social media engagement, and evaluate the effectiveness of your campaigns. These resources provide valuable insights into user behaviour and campaign performance, enabling you to make data-driven decisions.

Track Conversions:

Tracking conversions is fundamental for evaluating the success of your marketing campaigns. A conversion refers to any desired action you want your audience to take, such as submitting a form, making a purchase, or signing up for your email list. By monitoring conversion data, you can identify which strategies are effective and which ones need enhancement. This information helps you optimise your marketing activities and maximise your ROI.

Monitor Social Media Engagement:

Social media platforms offer an effective means of reaching and engaging your audience. To understand what resonates with your target demographic, it is essential to monitor and analyse your social media activities. Track metrics such as likes, shares, comments, and growth in followers and subscribers using analytics tools specific to each platform. This data provides insights into the forms of material and methods that are generating engagement, enabling you to refine your social media marketing approach.

Review Your Data Frequently:

Monitoring and evaluating your promotion initiatives requires you to frequently review your data. Every week or month, set aside time to study your analytics and determine what is and is not performing. By consistently inspecting your data, you can identify patterns, trends, and areas for improvement. This allows you to make informed decisions and adjust your marketing strategies for optimal results.

It might be time to change your methods if you see that some tactics are not yielding the desired results. On the other hand, if you discover that some of your campaigns are performing particularly well, you might want to think about allocating more funds to those strategies to increase your ROI. Keep an open mind and be prepared to test out new concepts to see what works best for your Brand Art.

FROM FART TO ART

Brand Fart

Photographers commit costly mistakes by failing to monitor and evaluate marketing initiatives. You run the risk of squandering time and money on ineffective promotion tactics that do not appeal to your target audience if you do not track conversions, keep an eye on social media engagement, and analyse your online data.

Brand Art

Marketing efforts must be measured and analysed for a photography brand to succeed. By setting clear goals, using analytics tools, and regularly reviewing data, you can make informed decisions about your advertisement strategies and build a brand that resonates with your target audience.

BRAND FART EVOLUTION

⌐¬
L ⌐

If you want to maintain relevance and appeal to your target demographic in the fiercely competitive photography market of today, it's essential to constantly evolve your brand. Your photography business should transform over time to reflect your current vision, values, and artistic expression. However, many photographers make common Brand Farts that damage their reputation during the process of developing their identity.

As a boudoir photographer, I've experienced firsthand the transformative power of a single photograph and how it has the power to make women feel seen, heard, and beautiful, regardless of their background. This revelation has pushed and inspired me to continuously evolve my brand and stay relevant and adaptable in a rapidly changing industry. For instance, I coined the phrase "Norteygraphy" to set my brand apart from others in my niche. This name is a play on my last name "Nortey" and best describes what I do as a creative and my editing style at the intersection of boudoir and photography.

This straightforward yet powerful one-word directs in upholding consistency in my brand identity, which is essential to fostering brand recognition and winning over my audience's trust. Having a clear and concise brand persona will enable me to stay focused on my niche and style as my brand evolves in response to any technological advancements, and prevent dilution by attempting to appeal to a wider demographic.

This helps build a loyal network of clients who appreciate my unique style and approach to boudoir photography, and creates a cohesive and memorable brand that resonates with my target market. Additionally, having a one-word brand identity can make it simpler for potential customers to find me online through search engines and social media platforms. Overall, cultivating a strong and clear artistic tagline is not only essential for any photographer aiming to stand out in a crowded sector and attract their ideal clients, but it also becomes the backbone for your brand evolution, allowing you to adapt and grow whilst preserving the core essence that differentiates you in the ever-changing creative industry.

In addition to the significance of brand evolution, the use of technology is another factor that photographers must consider to remain relevant in the market. One major development in the world of photography is the rise of Artificial Intelligence (AI) and its applications in the industry. Photographers can use AI to automate their workflows, enhance the quality of their images, and even create new visual content. Leveraging AI can give photographers a competitive advantage by allowing them to work faster and more efficiently.

Another development that has caught the attention of photographers is the emergence of Non-Fungible Tokens (NFTs). NFTs are a new type of digital asset that can be used to represent ownership of unique items, such as photographs. By giving photographers the ability to sell their images as unique, one-of-a-kind assets, this technology has the potential to completely change how photographers market and sell their work. By embracing NFTs, photographers can reach new audiences, gain more exposure, and increase the value of their work.

This chapter will cover how photographers can adapt to new technologies to grow their brands and maintain relevance in the competitive photography market. We'll also look at how to steer clear of common brand evolution blunders like failing to incorporate market trends and not embracing new techniques. Instead of falling into the trap of a static, out-of-date, Brand Fart that struggles to connect with your audience, you must create Brand Art that changes with the times and embodies your goals and personality. By adopting the latter and avoiding the former, you can make sure that your brand stays vibrant, competitive, and appealing to your target demographic.

FART/27:

Underestimating the Importance of Continuous Improvement and Evolution

Photographers must be willing to continually develop their craft and marketing methods in the industry's rapidly evolving landscape. To stay competitive and relevant, you must continually improve your photography techniques and business strategies. This is known as the process of continuous improvement and evolution.

But Why is it So Important for Photographers to Constantly Improve and Evolve?

Keeping updated with the most recent trends, technologies, and techniques, offering something unique and innovative, and championing personal development and contentment are just a few advantages of continuous improvement and evolution. Photography professionals can distinguish themselves in a crowded industry and provide fresh perspectives that clients may crave by constantly honing their skills and discovering new ways to market their creativity.

On the other hand, photographers who fail to evolve run the risk of losing relevance in the industry and becoming outdated. For instance, photographers who solely relied on film and conventional development methods found it difficult to compete in the digital age. On the flip side, photographers who embraced digital technology and fresh editing methods prospered.

The long-term viability of a photography business depends on continuous improvement and evolution. Photographers who regularly review and enhance their business models can pinpoint areas for development, streamline their operations, and adjust to shifting market dynamics. This enables you to build a resilient and flexible creative company that can flourish in various economic conditions and overcome obstacles.

Additionally, improvement and evolution are catalysts for personal and professional growth in the world of photography. They present photographers with valuable opportunities to broaden their knowledge, nurture new skills, and push the boundaries of their imagination. Photographers who actively embrace learning and development can not only experience greater fulfilment and satisfaction in their work but also establish themselves as respected and prosperous professionals in their areas of expertise. Continuous enhancement enables you to remain relevant, adjust to shifting consumer demands, and consistently provide your clients with exceptional results. Ultimately, the commitment to ongoing progress and evolution serves as a cornerstone for long-term success and the cultivation of a stellar reputation within and outside of the photography community.

Why Do Photographers Neglect Continuous Improvement and Evolution?

Belief in Current Abilities:

One reason photographers may disregard ongoing improvement and evolution is the belief that their current skills and abilities are already sufficient to meet the demands of the market. They might believe that they are competent at their current level and that they do not need to spend time and energy improving. However, this mindset can be detrimental in the long run. New trends, techniques, and consumer preferences emerge frequently in the dynamic, ever-evolving business of photography. By solely relying on your existing skill set, you risk falling behind competitors who actively seek to improve and adapt. Continuous learning and growth are essential to staying relevant and meeting the ever-changing demands of the market.

Reluctance to Embrace Change:

Some photographers may be resistant to change and find it difficult to adapt to new technologies and techniques. They may have become comfortable with their current methods and feel apprehensive about incorporating unfamiliar tools or approaches into their workflow. However, failing to be open to innovation can hinder your progress and limit your growth potential. New technologies and techniques can enhance efficiency, expand creative possibilities, and improve the overall quality of your work. Photographers can stay ahead of the curve and provide distinctive and compelling services to their clients by embracing change and being willing to learn and implement modern processes.

Lack of Industry Awareness:

Lack of awareness of the implications of industry technological shifts is another factor contributing to photographers' potential neglect of continuous improvement and evolution. They may not fully grasp the impact that staying stagnant can have on their business. The photography market is extremely competitive, and customers are always looking for fresh perspectives. By failing to actively keep up with industry trends and developments, you risk becoming outdated and losing relevance in the market.

Limited Resources for Development:

The ability of photographers to focus on ongoing development and evolution can also be hampered by practical limitations like a lack of funds, time, or resources. Workshops, training programmes, and equipment upgrades can require financial investments and time commitments that may not always be readily available. However, you need to recognise that investing in your professional development is an expenditure for the long-term success of your business. Exploring alternative options, such as free online courses, webinars, or networking events, can provide accessible and cost-effective avenues for learning and growth.

So How Can Photographers Improve and Evolve?

There are numerous workshops and educational programmes available that accommodate photographers of all skill levels. These events provide a valuable opportunity to hear from industry experts, gain insights into the latest trends, and receive hands-on training. By immersing yourself in these learning environments, you can expand your knowledge, refine your techniques, and discover new avenues for expressing your artistic vision.

Furthermore, there is a wealth of wisdom accessible through photography-focused blogs, magazines, and social media channels. You can get useful information, find inspiration, and keep up with the most recent developments in the industry by actively consuming these resources. Following influential photographers and engaging in online communities and forums can foster a sense of connection and provide opportunities for exchanging ideas and personal growth.

Seeking mentorship or collaborating with fellow creatives can also be immensely beneficial. Mentors and seasoned photographers can offer guidance and support, assisting you in overcoming obstacles and broadening your horizons. Collaborations and partnerships provide opportunities for learning from one another and advancing together without placing an excessive strain on your resources.

Additionally, actively seeking feedback from trustworthy peers and industry professionals can provide priceless insights for improvement. Their constructive critique can help you identify areas of strength and areas that need further development, ultimately helping you refine your skills and elevate your photography to new heights.

It's crucial to realise that evolution and continuous improvement are essential components of building a fruitful and long-lasting brand as a photographer. Embracing change, being receptive to new ideas, and remaining adaptable is key to staying ahead of the curve and unlocking your full potential in the dynamic photography industry. Keep in mind, the process of evolving your brand does not entail a complete overhaul of what you already excel at, but rather, it involves fine-tuning and adapting to meet the changing market demands and preferences of your target audience. By acknowledging and addressing potential barriers, such as limited resources or a lack of industry development awareness, and actively prioritising continuous improvement, photographers can overcome challenges and propel themselves towards growth and success.

SUMMARY:

FROM FART TO ART

Brand Fart

Photographers are in danger of becoming stagnant and limiting their growth potential if they neglect constant evolution and improvement. Choosing not to keep up with new technologies and market trends can lead to decreased client satisfaction and business loss. It will become difficult to compete with other photographers in your niche if you don't develop your skills and evolve with the times.

Brand Art

Success in the highly competitive photography industry depends on constant evolution and improvement. You can maintain relevance and deliver value to your clients by consistently developing your abilities, picking up new skills, and adjusting to technological changes. Embracing these fundamental principles not only enhances your craft but also opens up new business opportunities and boosts customer satisfaction.

FART/28:

Not Staying Relevant and Adaptable

In the rapidly changing field of photography, success is contingent upon being relevant and adaptable. Keeping on top of new gear and software, marketing techniques, and industry practices, as well as being flexible to changing client needs, is crucial. Failure to stay updated with the latest trends and developments in the industry can lead to missed opportunities and lost business.

Photographer Annie Leibovitz's long and illustrious career illustrates the importance of remaining relevant and adaptable in an industry that experiences abrupt shifts. Her willingness to adopt new technologies and techniques as they emerged whilst maintaining her creative vision and style has been one of the pillars of her success.

Annie Leibovitz is an American photographer who is famed for her work in portrait photography. She started her career working as a staff photographer for Rolling Stone magazine in the 1970s, when photography was quickly transitioning from a traditional craft to a more modern art form. She was one of the pioneering photographers to experiment with cutting-edge methods like colour saturation and unconventional lighting, and editors and publishers were quick to notice her fresh perspective.

Annie worked for a number of publications over the years, including Vanity Fair and Vogue, and photographed a variety of individuals, including politicians, celebrities, and cultural icons. She became one of the most sought-after photographers in the world thanks to her distinctive vivid glamour aesthetic, which frequently incorporates her subjects in predetermined positions.

Some of Annie's most famous photographs include a portrait of a pregnant Demi Moore for the cover of Vanity Fair in 1991, a series of images of Queen Elizabeth II in 2007 and the Queen's 90th birthday in 2016, and iconic pictures of musicians such as John Lennon and Bruce Springsteen.

Annie's success can be attributed to her capacity to adapt to the changing environment as the industry continued to evolve by persistently looking for new opportunities and challenges. She expanded into different photographic fields like fashion and advertising and started looking into the potential of digital imaging and other innovative technologies at the time.

Despite her success, Annie has consistently stayed true to her distinct aesthetic, which is characterised by her visual storytelling and a keen eye for detail. Her versatility and adaptability whilst upholding the integrity of her artistic vision are a testament to her creativity, talent, and commitment to her craft.

Annie's most recent work has kept on pushing the limits of photography by utilising the latest techniques and tools to produce breathtaking pictures that are both conceptually brilliant and emotionally stirring. She has also continued to collaborate with a wide range of clients, from household-name celebrities to everyday people, ensuring that her work remains relevant and accessible to a diverse audience.

Keeping Up with Technology

It's critical that you stay up-to date with changes in camera advancements, editing software, and post-processing methods, because these developments are evolving constantly. Make it a point to research and incorporate emerging technologies, like AI and NFTs. Keep in mind, new technology doesn't care about your opinion of whether it's a good or bad thing for the industry. If you don't utilise the benefits, you will lose out.

Here are some key strategies to help you stay ahead of the curve.

The Influence of Social Media Trends and Algorithms:
A social media presence alone is not sufficient. For photographers to fully utilise these platforms and maximise their online marketing efforts, they must stay current with the latest social media trends and algorithms.

Keeping up with and leveraging social media trends is an important strategy that photographers must employ. The features, algorithms, and content formats on social media platforms are constantly changing. Photographers can modify their material and marketing methods by keeping a close eye on these developments. Maintaining relevance and meaningful engagement with your audience requires you to stay on top of online advancements, whether it's embracing the rise of video content, taking advantage of TikTok's popularity, or exploring the potential of emerging platforms.

Another essential component of effective online marketing is having a solid understanding of social media algorithms. Using criteria like relevance, engagement, and audience preferences, algorithms decide what content users see in their feeds. Photographers need to become familiar with these algorithms in order to tailor their material and maximise their reach and visibility. This may entail producing engaging and high-quality posts, utilising relevant hashtags, encouraging interactions, and posting frequently. By aligning your strategies with social media algorithms, you can increase your chances of reaching a larger audience and gaining exposure.

In today's digital environment, it is crucial for photographers to embrace social media trends and algorithms. Your online marketing efforts could suffer significantly if you choose to ignore these developments. Ultimately, you are in danger of your content becoming stagnant and less visible to your target audience if you fail to stay updated. As social media platforms prioritise engaging and relevant material, photographers who fail to adapt may experience a decline in organic reach and interaction, making it harder to attract new clients and grow their businesses.

Photographers who utilise social media trends and algorithms, however, gain a competitive advantage. By leveraging these trends, you can showcase your creativity, experiment with different content formats, and connect with your market on a deeper level. You can benefit from features such as live streaming, interactive stories, and user-generated material to cultivate a sense of community and authenticity. Understanding algorithms also enables photographers to improve their artistic strategy, boost engagement, and develop a devoted fan base. This can lead to greater brand awareness, more enquiries, and ultimately, a flourishing photography business.

Unleashing the Power of NFTs:

Non-Fungible Tokens (NFTs) have emerged as groundbreaking technology that has significant implications for photographers and their business models. Embracing NFTs can provide photographers with unique opportunities to monetise their work, establish ownership, and connect with a global audience in the digital realm.

This technological innovation allows photographers to mint their photos as NFTs to establish digital ownership and authenticity, preventing their work from being copied or altered without their permission. Ultimately, this creates a sense of exclusivity and scarcity around your art, potentially increasing its value and desirability among collectors.

One strategy photographers can implement is participating in NFT marketplaces and auctions. Bypassing conventional middlemen, these platforms enable photographers to showcase and sell their NFTs directly to collectors. By leveraging the decentralised nature of blockchain technology, you can reach a global audience and potentially earn royalties whenever your NFTs are resold. This direct connection with buyers and the potential for ongoing revenue streams can significantly impact photographers' financial sustainability and independence.

Photographers can also explore partnerships and collaborations with digital artists. By teaming up with creators in the space, photographers can leverage their respective audiences and expertise to produce unique NFT projects that combine photography with other digital art forms. This can lead to innovative and visually compelling artworks that attract attention, generate buzz, and open up new avenues for exposure and financial rewards.

On the other hand, photographers who choose to neglect NFT technology may face challenges in protecting their digital assets and commercialising their work effectively. Collectors and buyers are increasingly drawn to the digital world in search of distinctive and authenticated works of art. By opting to reject NFTs, you risk missing out on this emerging market, thus reducing your scope for growth and monetary success.

For photographers to adjust to the evolving landscape of digital art and ownership, they must explore integrating NFT technology. The demand for digital collectibles and NFTs has skyrocketed, attracting art enthusiasts, and investors, from around the globe. By adopting NFTs, you put yourself at the forefront of this revolutionary technology, showcasing your forward-thinking attitude and eagerness for navigating uncharted waters in the industry.

Embracing the AI Revolution:
Artificial intelligence (AI) has transformed the creative process and opened up new possibilities in the field of photography. Photographers can benefit significantly from adopting AI technology in the realm of image creation, allowing them to push the envelope, elevate their artistic vision, and deliver remarkable end products.

Making use of AI-powered photo enhancement tools is an approach that photographers can utilise. These tools leverage the use of sophisticated algorithms to analyse and modify a number of image characteristics, including colour balance, exposure, and sharpness. By incorporating AI into your creative process, you can achieve stunning results with minimal effort, saving time and ensuring consistent quality in your work.

A further option is exploring AI-generated content. AI programs have the ability to create images, mimic artistic techniques, and offer unique perspectives. Photographers can capitalise on this technology by using AI-generated pictures as a source of inspiration, incorporating AI-generated elements into their photographic works, or even working with AI systems to create unconventional and novel artworks. You can push the limits of your imagination to produce striking and thought-provoking visuals.

Additionally, AI's style transfer algorithms can help photographers explore innovative avenues. With the help of these algorithms, which analyse one image's style and apply it to another, photographers can experiment with various artistic approaches and produce works that are both visually breathtaking and unique. By utilising AI-powered design transfer, you can expand your creative spectrum, offer clients a broader range of options, and cater to diverse aesthetic preferences in your niche.

To remain relevant and competitive in an industry that is changing rapidly, photographers must integrate AI technology into their creative processes. From content creation to image editing, AI is being incorporated into more and more aspects of photography. You could experience limitations in terms of productivity, artistic exploration, and meeting changing client demands if you refuse to implement AI into your expressive workflow.

By embracing AI, creators put themselves at the forefront of the industry's innovation and technological advancements. They can leverage AI to explore new techniques, experiment with cutting-edge tools, and push the boundaries of traditional photography. Photographers who welcome AI will be able to show that they are adaptable, have a forward-looking outlook, and are open to deploying new technologies.

SUMMARY:

FROM FART TO ART

Brand Fart

Failing to stay relevant and adaptable in the rapidly evolving photography industry can have detrimental effects on a photographer's success. By neglecting to keep up with emerging trends, technological advancements, and changing client preferences, you risk falling behind and missing valuable business opportunities. Disregarding the significance of social media developments and algorithms, overlooking the potential of AI technology, and dismissing the possibilities offered by NFTs can result in limited market reach, an inability to meet the changing demands of customers, and a weakened brand positioning.

Brand Art

In the rapidly evolving photography industry, success hinges on staying current and adaptable. By proactively engaging with social media trends and algorithms, embracing AI technology, and exploring NFTs, photographers can enhance their online presence, attract a larger audience, and thrive in the dynamic landscape of the industry. Staying up-to-date and flexible empowers you to seize new opportunities, connect with a global audience, and establish your presence in the digital art space. Adopting these strategies enables you to position yourself for success, foster business growth, and make a significant impact in the photographic industry.

FINAL THOUGHTS

Entering Competitions to Elevate Your Brand Art

┌ ┐
└ ┘

We have discussed the significance of brand niching, messaging, marketing, pricing, and evolution in the chapters of this book, as well as how these elements work in tandem to communicate your unique value proposition and distinguish you from your competitors. However, you might now be wondering how to elevate your brand further and increase market visibility. Participating in photography competitions serves as an effective strategy.

Entering photography competitions offers a range of benefits for photographers looking to strengthen their Brand Art. Here are some reasons why.

Exposure to New Audiences:

The publicity your brand can receive from competing in photography contests is one of the biggest advantages. Whether they take place online or in person, competitions frequently draw lots of spectators, and this can help your work reach new audiences that it might not have otherwise. Your photographs can gain significant exposure and contribute to the development of your professional reputation by winning or even just being chosen as a finalist in a competition. Such visibility may result in media attention, joint venture possibilities, and ultimately more demand for your photographic services.

Validation of Your Talent:

When you enter a photography competition, you are putting your artwork up against that of other talented creatives. This can be intimidating, but if your photos are acknowledged and rewarded, it can also feel incredibly validating. Winning or placing in a competition can also be a great way to show potential clients your abilities and expertise and help to establish your brand's credibility.

Networking Opportunities:

Photography competitions can offer beneficial networking opportunities in addition to exposure and validation. The chance to connect with other photographers, judges, and industry leaders may result in new business partnerships or even employment prospects. Any successful brand requires interpersonal relationships, and participating in competitions can help you grow your network of professional contacts.

Feedback and Critique:
When you enter a competition, you'll often receive feedback and critique from judges and other photographers. This can be extremely valuable in helping you enhance your photographic skills and refine your editing style. Even if you don't win, the constructive criticism you obtain will help you improve as a photographer and can be used to guide your future work.

Now, it's important to note that not all photography competitions are created the same. You should carefully consider which challenges are worth your time and money by doing your research and making informed decisions. Find contests that fit your preferences and interests, provide worthwhile exposure or prizes, and have a reputable judging panel.

While participating in competitions can be a great way to get recognition and publicity, it also exposes you and your work to criticism. The truth is that not everyone will like your photography approach or aesthetic, and you may face rejection. This can be disheartening, but it's important to remember that getting overlooked and your style being misunderstood is a natural part of the creative process and shouldn't be taken personally.

Additionally, take into account the cost of entry and the time commitment involved. Entering competitions can be time-consuming and expensive, so it's important to weigh the potential benefits against the financial implications and determine whether it's a worthwhile investment for your brand. The time and money you might have spent on marketing, client work, or personal projects could be diverted by competing in various contests.

It's important to keep in mind that participating in competitions shouldn't be viewed as the end goal in and of itself, but rather as a tool for strengthening your brand identity. If you're not careful, it's easy to become preoccupied with competing and lose sight of your creative career vision and objectives. Remember to stay true to your photographic style and philosophy, and use competitions as a way to gain exposure, validation, and feedback while continuing to develop your own unique Brand Art. By strategically entering competitions and leveraging the benefits they provide, you can elevate your brand and stand out in an already saturated marketplace.

Embracing Your Greatness

My journey behind the camera has been like riding a roller coaster with ups and downs. However, it has ultimately led me to recognise the importance of branding and the role it plays in achieving success both within and outside of the creative industry.

Through my foray into photography and research into personal branding, it became apparent that there was a gap in the market for household-name photographers. I firmly believe that together with my peers we can shatter the glass ceiling and achieve the same level of accomplishments and acclaim as other greats in various artistic fields with the right combination of skill, originality, and effective branding.

To become a successful photographer, it's important to remember that it's not just about taking great photos. You must also understand the business side of things well to make wise choices about how to present yourself and your work to the world.

Unfortunately, a lot of photographers make the mistake of concentrating too much on surface-level Brand Fart components, rather than on the core elements of creating a wholly authentic Brand Art identity. These photographers ultimately find themselves struggling to stand out from the competition and leave a lasting impression on the industry.

The evolution of social networks into Collectively Conscious Consumer Communities has transferred the authority to shape a company's brand image from businesses to consumers. This shift emphasises the importance of photographers proactively managing their brand reputation. While you cannot control how individuals emotionally connect with your brand, you do have the ability to guide the general public's perception of your business by providing exceptional service and upholding a robust, authentic brand narrative.

At the heart of building a flourishing brand as a creative is the need to embrace your true potential as a Brand Art photographer. Being clear about who you are, what you have to offer, and how you want to be viewed in the marketplace is necessary for this. Both as an artist and a businessperson, it takes commitment, hard work, and a willingness to constantly develop and get better.

It's important to first establish your definition of success in order to thrive. Is it landing a certain type of client, shooting for a specific publication, or simply making a comfortable living doing something you love? Whatever it may be, setting achievable goals is key to reaching the summit of your career mountain.

Making a mark, however, involves more than simply crossing goals off a list. It's about pushing yourself to achieve your maximum potential and continually seeking new ways to improve your craft. This entails looking for fresh development opportunities, whether that's by attending workshops and conferences, collaborating with other creatives, or experimenting with new techniques and equipment.

Whilst striving for excellence is important, it's equally crucial to keep in mind that being the best photographer in your field is not the objective. It's about being the best version of your creative self. Instead of comparing yourself to others, you should concentrate on your own personal growth and development. By implementing your style and vision, you can establish a unique niche for yourself in the industry and utilise it to create meaningful and impactful work.

Achieving longevity in the photography industry hinges on striking a delicate balance between financial goals and artistic integrity. It is important to approach this balance cautiously and resist the temptation to be driven solely by monetary gain. While achieving financial success is undoubtedly important for operating a photography business, focusing solely on income can have adverse consequences. Remember, genuine success in photography is not solely measured by money earned but also by the ability to authentically express your creativity and forge meaningful connections with those who appreciate and value your unique perspective as a photographer.

Ultimately, your ascent up the rocky terrain of photography is not a race to the top, financially or artistically, but a journey of self-discovery and growth. So, whether you're just starting or have been climbing for years, take the time to appreciate the view along the way and celebrate the small victories that lead to your goal apex.

I have shared with you the importance of establishing your brand's identity, pinpointing your niche, and creating an appealing visual brand. Beyond these observable aspects of branding, it's vital to pay attention to the intangible elements that truly define your Brand Art – your distinct vision, photographic philosophy, and personality that sets you apart from the competition.

You can establish a strong emotional bond with your audience and develop a brand that is both genuine and memorable by fully embracing your uniqueness and expressing it through your work.

Instead of attempting to appeal to everyone, honing in on a particular niche allows you to become a sought-after expert in that specific field. By defining your unique value proposition and zeroing in on a unique style, genre, or demographic, you can position yourself as the go-to photographer for clients seeking your specialised expertise. Understanding your strengths and adopting a focused approach not only gives you a competitive advantage against photographers who are broadminded, but also allows you to establish a reputation for excellence and mastery in your chosen discipline, making it easier to attract your ideal customer base and build a healthy photography business.

Your photo editing choices, whether showcasing bold and vibrant colours or employing a soft and ethereal aesthetic, contribute to the overall storytelling of your brand. This strategic approach effectively communicates your creative vision and helps you differentiate yourself as a photographer. Consistently applying your post-processing style throughout your workflow allows you to create a unified and recognisable visual identity that resonates with your intended audience. By crafting a distinctive brand message through your retouching technique, you can efficiently convey your unique perspective and attract clients who appreciate your artistic trademark.

Shifting your priority from charging solely based on time to the value and impact of the services you deliver can dramatically elevate your brand and financial success. Keeping in mind that clients are not simply paying for the hours you spend behind the camera, but for the expertise, imagination, and individual perspective you bring to their projects, you can position yourself as a valuable asset in their eyes.

This adjustment allows you to align your pricing with the value you provide, ensuring that your talents are fairly compensated and appreciated by clients who seek exceptional quality and a distinctive artistic vision. By focusing on pricing and business model practices that emphasise your worth, you can not only enhance your profitability but also communicate your professionalism and commitment to delivering unparalleled results.

To differentiate yourself as a photographer in today's highly competitive industry, you must also use social media and other online platforms to share your work and interact with potential clients. However, it's important to remember that social media should be used as a tool to enhance your Brand Art, not as a substitute for it. Always prioritise your Brand Art on web channels you control, such as your personal website or blog, and use social networks to amplify and promote it.

Throughout history, there have been many photographers who did not adapt to new technologies. For instance, when digital photography first emerged in the late 20th century, many photographers chose not to embrace it, and they were left behind by those who did. When Adobe Photoshop was first introduced, the same situation transpired. Those who refused to accept it were at a disadvantage. Photographers who do not adopt new technologies run the risk of becoming irrelevant, and may lose clients to those who have done so.

As photography enters a new technological era, building a strong Brand Art that distinguishes you from what artificial intelligence can produce is more important than ever as the technology develops. The reality is, if AI can replicate your photographic work for less, your photography business could be rendered obsolete. Regardless of your stance on AI, it is clear that technology will continue to play a significant role in the creative industry. Therefore, you must adapt, find new ways to stand out, and carve out a specific market niche if you want to stay relevant.

Building a fruitful brand as a photographer also requires networking and forming strong bonds with other industry peers. By collaborating with photographers, models, makeup artists, influencers, and other professionals, you can not only expand your circle of connections but also gain valuable insights and inspiration that can help you grow as a creative.

Becoming an influential photographer requires persistence, patience, and effort. But by focusing on your Brand Art and avoiding the superficial Brand Fart elements, you can set yourself up for success and create a path towards a rewarding and long-lasting profession. Always keep in mind that the road to becoming a prosperous and recognisable photographer is a continuous process of self-discovery, experimentation, and improvement, regardless of whether you're at the beginning of your journey or looking to re-evaluate and revamp your approach.

Photography has transformed my life in ways I never imagined possible. I was struggling with depression and feeling directionless, but the day I was gifted a camera, everything changed for the better. Now that I've discovered my creative calling in this amazing industry that I'm genuinely passionate about, I wake up every morning feeling content and happy.

The opportunity to travel and interact with incredibly talented individuals is one of the most thrilling aspects of being a photographer. I'm grateful for all the connections I've made with fellow photographers, models, and other creative professionals, here in the UK and abroad, as they have taught me so much and helped me grow as an artist. Through my industry collaborations, I met my best friend on a photoshoot, who became the love of my life. She's my biggest cheerleader, support, and inspiration.

In a relatively short period, photography has given me so much and has truly blessed my life in countless ways. For this reason, I felt a strong desire to give back, starting with sharing my knowledge and expertise in this book.

Photography is more than just taking the perfect picture. It is an art form that deserves to be honoured as such. I'm now on a personal mission to change how people both inside and outside of the creative industry view photography, but I'm well aware that it will require cooperation from my photographer peers to accomplish this.

To move forward together as a community, I want to encourage you to unlock your inherent capabilities as a branded photographer by concentrating on your Brand Art, expressing it through your work, and utilising social media to amplify your message. By following the steps outlined in this book, don't be afraid to take risks, try new things, and be true to yourself. With hard work, determination, a willingness to continuously evolve and adapt, and a thirst to maximise your full potential, you can turn your passion for photography into a thriving and fulfilling career.

Your Next Chapter

You have finished reading the book. However, this marks the beginning of your journey towards crafting a remarkable photography brand.

Head over to **BrandFart.com** for a range of valuable resources, including informative blog posts, courses, and workshops designed to help you create a successful brand.

Take advantage of our exclusive Brand Fart test tool to assess whether your photographic brand needs some fine-tuning or is already a work of Brand Art.

Don't wait - visit **BrandFart.com** today and unlock the full potential of your creative brand!

SCAN ME

Brand Art: Case Studies

THE SEARCH FOR GREATNESS: MY STORY

Kai Wong

www.kaimanwong.com

www.instagram.com/kaimanwong

www.youtube.com/@KaiManWong

BRAND NICHING

Brandon Woelfel

www.brandonwoelfel.com

www.instagram.com/brandonwoelfel

www.youtube.com/@BrandonWoelfel

BRAND MESSAGING

Badboi

www.matabad.com

www.instagram.com/badboi

BRAND PRICING

Ryan and Tatiana Brenizer

www.thebrenizers.com

www.instagram.com/thebrenizers

BRAND MARKETING

Jessica Kobeissi

www.jessicakobeissi.com

www.instagram.com/jessicakobeissi

www.youtube.com/@JessicaKobeissi

BRAND EVOLUTION

Annie Leibovitz

www.instagram.com/annieleibovitz

About the Author

In mid-2014, Neo 'Norteyrazzi' Nortey stumbled upon 'DigitalRev TV,' a popular photography YouTube channel hosted by Kai Wong, and was instantly captivated. Despite never owning a digital camera, he knew that he had found his calling in the creative field. Nevertheless, Norteyrazzi ended up pursuing a different career path at the time.

However, everything changed in February 2019 when he expressed his desire to delve into photography to a family friend. She generously gifted Norteyrazzi her unused Canon 1100D camera, and after practising at home and photographing a couple of events, he finally took a leap of faith and had his first photoshoot with a model in early August 2019 in Central London. That marked the beginning of a fulfilling photography journey, and he hasn't looked back since.

As a boudoir photographer, Norteyrazzi's distinctive photographic process, which he calls "Norteygraphy," has earned him widespread recognition and admiration. His portfolio features breathtaking images of numerous beautiful women, and he is renowned for having helped launch the careers of countless aspiring models. His artistic vision has taken him on a journey through Europe, where he worked with several boutique brands to produce visually stunning imagery that has captured the attention of viewers worldwide.

Tweet

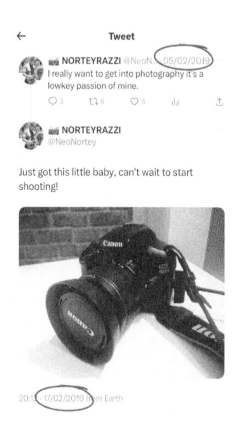

NORTEYRAZZI @NeoN... 05/02/2019
I really want to get into photography it's a
lowkey passion of mine.

♡ 3   ↻ 6   ♡ 6   ᵢₗᵢ   ⬆

NORTEYRAZZI
@NeoNortey

Just got this little baby, can't wait to start
shooting!

20:1? · 17/02/2019 from Earth

Support The Author

Review Brand Fart on **Amazon**

Subscribe to **YouTube** Channel: www.youtube.com/@norteyrazzi

Follow on **Instagram:** www.instagram.com/norteyrazzi

Connect on **X:** www.x.com/neonortey

Follow on **TikTok:** www.tiktok.com/@norteyrazzi

View portfolio on **Website:** www.norteyrazzi.com

Acknowledgement

Without My Lord and Saviour Jesus Christ, this book would not have been possible.

(Luke 1:37)

Copyright

Copyright © 2023 Neo Nortey 'Norteyrazzi'. All rights reserved.

This notice applies to the book "Brand Fart - Avoiding The 28 Common Branding Mistakes Photographers Make" and all content contained therein. No part of this book may be reproduced, distributed, or transmitted in any form or by any means, including photocopying, recording, or other electronic or mechanical methods, without the prior written permission of the author, except in the case of brief quotations embodied in critical reviews and certain other non-commercial uses permitted by copyright law.

This publication is protected by the copyright laws of the United Kingdom and international treaties. Any unauthorised reproduction, distribution or use of this book is prohibited and may result in both civil and criminal penalties.

ISBN: 978-1-3999-6564-4

For permission requests or further information, please contact the author at the following email address: info@brandfart.com.

www.brandfart.com
www.norteyrazzi.com

Printed in Great Britain
by Amazon

41954258R00145